Destiny vs Free Will

Destiny vs Free Will

Why Things Happen the Way They Do

David R. Hamilton, PhD

HAY HOUSE

Australia • Canada • Hong Kong • India
South Africa • United Kingdom • United States

First published and distributed in the United Kingdom by:
Hay House UK Ltd, 292B Kensal Rd, London W10 5BE.
Tel.: (44) 20 8962 1230; Fax: (44) 20 8962 1239. www.hayhouse.co.uk

Published and distributed in the United States of America by:
Hay House, Inc., PO Box 5100, Carlsbad, CA 92018-5100.
Tel.: (1) 760 431 7695 or (800) 654 5126;
Fax: (1) 760 431 6948 or (800) 650 5115. www.hayhouse.com

Published and distributed in Australia by:
Hay House Australia Ltd, 18/36 Ralph St, Alexandria NSW 2015.
Tel.: (61) 2 9669 4299; Fax: (61) 2 9669 4144. www.hayhouse.com.au

Published and distributed in the Republic of South Africa by:
Hay House SA (Pty), Ltd, PO Box 990, Witkoppen 2068.
Tel./Fax: (27) 11 706 6612. orders@psdprom.co.za

Published and distributed in India by:
Hay House Publishers India, Muskaan Complex, Plot No.3,
B-2, Vasant Kunj, New Delhi – 110 070.
Tel.: (91) 11 41761620; Fax: (91) 11 41761630. www.hayhouse.co.in

Distributed in Canada by:
Raincoast, 9050 Shaughnessy St, Vancouver, BC V6P 6E5.
Tel.: (1) 604 323 7100; Fax: (1) 604 323 2600

A catalogue record for this book is available from the British Library.

ISBN 978-1-4019-1569-8

Printed and bound in the UK by CPI Mackays, Chatham ME5 8TD

For Elizabeth...

*Your constant love and support have made this book
possible. Thank you from the bottom of my heart.*

Contents

Acknowledgements

First and foremost, I would like to thank my partner Elizabeth Caproni for being a constant source of inspiration, wisdom and support and for reading through and advising me on every chapter.

I am also grateful for the love and support that I constantly receive from all the members of both my family and Elizabeth's.

I would also like to thank Michelle Pilley, Jo Burgess and all the staff at Hay House UK for having faith in me.

To my editor, Lizzie Hutchins, a big thank you for taking what I'd written and shaping it into an easier-to-read and coherent whole.

For insights into astrology I would like to thank Shelley von Strunckel.

I would like to thank everyone who sent me details of their near-death experiences. In particular, I would like to thank Susan Scott, Mary Scott, Rachel Martin and Nancy Martin.

I would also like to thank Brian Weiss for information about our future.

For interesting discussions on life I would like to say thank you to Tyson Joseph.

Introduction

'It was meant to be.' That is a statement that I have heard hundreds of times. But are things really meant to be? How much influence does free will have? There are so many books nowadays showing us how we can create our own personal reality, but I have always felt that sometimes stuff just happens.

When I was growing up, one of the most commonly used phrases in the village was 'What's for you won't go by you.' As I started out with this book I had that phrase in mind. I wanted to look at the forces of destiny and free will.

In approaching the subject I first examined astrology, because it is often said that our lives are 'written in the stars'. I had never ventured into it before, though I had always wondered how an astrologer was able to look at a birth chart and see a person's whole life. Now I realize that a birth chart is a highly accurate map of the planets and stars at the moment of a person's birth. The skill of an astrologer is in interpreting the chart.

A birth chart is really like a storybook of symbols. Each planet and constellation has a myth or story associated with it that has been with us for thousands of years and has become imprinted on our collective psyche.

In the last century the great psychoanalyst Carl Jung popularized the concept of the collective unconscious, a repository of information that we all share. It is much like the Internet – we are all separate, just as individual computers are, but we share a common 'mind', just as computers share the Internet. So, as myths and stories become popular, they become available to us all at an unconscious level. Even if you haven't consciously learned about, say, the myth of Mars, the Roman god of war, you will know the story unconsciously. And furthermore, when the unconscious mind recognizes a story in the sky, which could be a planet entering a particular constellation of the zodiac, you begin to unconsciously play out that story in your own life.

As well as these archetypal stories in the sky, we are all affected by the sun, moon and planets via the Earth's magnetic field. Both human and animal nervous systems are sensitive to this field. Indeed, many animals rely on it to guide them on long migrations. So not only do the planets affect us through the stories that they symbolize in our unconscious minds, but they also have direct magnetic effects on our health and emotions. The scientific evidence for this is strong and compelling. But does this mean the planets and stars force behaviour upon us or does free will allow us to overrule their influence?

In addition to our cosmic destiny, we all have a biological destiny that we inherit from our parents. New evidence is showing that we inherit the consequences of the experiences of our parents, grandparents, great grand-parents and even earlier ancestors. Recent research in a field of science known as epigenetics has shown that life experiences alter our genes in such a way that the change is passed down to the next generation, and the one after that, and the one after that. So part of your genetic legacy stems from what happened to your parents, their parents and their parents before them. And your children and your children's children will bear the consequences of the lifestyle you lead today. What you do influences their destiny.

Is this genetic inheritance fixed or can we exert our free will to shape our health in any way we wish, regardless of what our ancestors did?

From a deeper perspective, do we have the free will to choose the family we are born into? There is a common worldwide belief that the soul chooses the life that it is about to live.

Recent scientific evidence of this has come from studies of people who have had so-called near-death experiences, where they have clinically died but been resuscitated and have returned with memories of the afterlife. Such reports are so numerous that leading cardiologists around the world are now investigating the phenomenon. Evidence for life after death has also come from people who have undergone psychiatric hypnotic regression.

Some of these studies have suggested that certain aspects of life are chosen before birth. Could it be that we are unconsciously guided by a memory of our pre-birth choices? Many people believe that certain subjects naturally inspire us because we 'remember' them and that we develop relationships with certain people because we planned to meet. Are such agreements fixed or can we change them along the way? Is everything that happens meant to happen? Or do we have the free will to create whatever we want, whatever the conditions we are born into and whatever our pre-birth choices might have been?

According to the law of attraction, we attract what we focus on. So we all have the power to attract what inspires us and makes us happy. What does this mean in terms of our destiny? Can we use our free will to change it by bringing new things into our lives?

On a global level, it has been suggested that the conditions of the world are the product of our collective choices. Do we have the power to change the direction in which the world is heading or are we locked into a preordained future?

The well-known psychiatrist and international bestselling author Dr Brian Weiss progressed thousands of patients into the future and many described a startlingly similar picture of the world 100–200 years from now, 300–600 years from now and 1,000 years from now.

Many indigenous cultures have prophecies about a change in the world that's due soon. Indeed, the Mayan calendar, which charts a cycle of 5,200 years, ends on 21 December 2012. The sun is also expected to reach a maximum level of solar activity in 2012. Are we destined for inevitable changes or could we choose what type of world we wish to live in?

Could it start with each of us – in our own hearts and minds?

David Hamilton
February 2007

Written in the Stars

When I was a child, the stars and planets fascinated me. I loved to read books about them. My earliest memories of knowing trivia was trivia about the planets – how long they took to rotate around the sun, how many moons they had, and so on. Even now, there are few things I find more relaxing than looking up at the stars on a clear night.

But is our destiny written in the stars, as astrologers have claimed? It is certainly true that the sun, moon and planets all have an effect on us. There is growing scientific evidence that they affect our hormones and emotions – and therefore our lives.

It has long been known that the moon's gravity tugs on the Earth and this gives us the oceans' tides. It also tugs on us and has both hormonal and behavioural effects. One of these is on the fertility cycles of women. In one scientific study of 826 women, 28 per cent were found to begin menstruating during the four days around the new moon, the phase where the moon is at its smallest and is beginning a new cycle, but no more than 13 per cent began menstruating during any other four-day period of the month.

A study published in the *Medical Journal of Australia* examined hospital admissions for self-poisoning around the time of a full moon, which is when the moon is at its largest, 14 days after a new moon. Looking at 2,215 admissions between 1988 and 1993, the researchers found that women were 25 per cent less likely to take an overdose around the time of a full moon than they were around the time of a new moon. They also found that at new moon women were more likely to overdose than men and at full moon men were more likely to overdose than women.

People have noticed the moon's ability to affect human behaviour for centuries. The werewolf myth comes from this. A number of mental health workers have also noted that the more disturbed a patient is, the greater the moon's effect on them. In 1842 the Lunacy Act in the UK actually defined a lunatic as someone who was 'rational during the first two phases of the moon and afflicted with a period of fatuity in the period following the full moon'.

Dr Frank Brown of Northwestern University, USA, found a correlation between the moon and the opening of oysters. He moved a group of oysters from Long Island Sound

1,000 miles inland to Evanson, Illinois. Initially, in darkened and pressurized tanks, the oysters continued to open and close their valves to the rhythms of the tides at Long Island. But after about two weeks they began to change. Their opening and closing rhythms began to synchronize with what they would be if there were tides in Evanson – in effect, they began to synchronize with the movement of the moon.

In the 1960s the French psychologist and statistician Michel Gauquelin found statistical evidence connecting the position of the moon and career choice. By correlating the position of the moon at the time of birth with profession, he discovered that statistically, distinguished writers or outstanding politicians tended to be born when the moon was at its highest point in the sky or when it was rising.

In 1966 Gauquelin expanded his research to include the effects of the planets. Using the same statistical methods, he checked the positions of certain planets at the time of birth of 576 members of the French Academy of Medicine. Astonishingly, he found that statistically they tended to be born when the planets Mars or Saturn had either just passed the highest point in the sky or were on the horizon.

Just to make absolutely sure that this wasn't just a coincidence, Gauquelin repeated the analysis with distinguished individuals from Germany, Holland, Italy, Belgium, the USA and Scotland, getting the same results each time.

There are two trains of thought as to exactly how the moon and the planets affect us. The first is through magnetism.

The magnetic tune

The Earth is a magnet – a very large one. And a magnet isn't just magnetic when you touch it with a piece of metal. Its magnetism extends a few inches out from it. This is its magnetic field. You can feel it when you hold a piece of metal a little way away from a magnet – you can feel the pull.

The Earth's magnetic field also extends out from it, and because of its relatively close proximity, the moon's movement affects it, causing it to fluctuate throughout the day. The human nervous system is sensitive to this field, so it is in turn influenced by the moon's behaviour.

The way that planets affect us is a little more subtle. To understand it, here's a little lesson in astronomy.

The moon rotates around the Earth every 29.5 days, being held in place by the Earth's gravity, which also makes apples fall off trees and means that when you jump up you come down again. The Earth and the other planets (Mercury, Venus, Mars, Jupiter, Saturn, Uranus, Neptune and the planetoid Pluto), all rotate around the sun, being held by its gravity. The time it takes for the Earth to go right around the sun and back to its starting-point is what we call one year.

The sun is an enormous ball of hot gas – so hot that it heats us up, even though we are 93 million miles away from it. There are constant explosions on it, as you would expect from something so big and hot, and every now and then if an explosion is severe enough, radiation is ejected outwards. Sometimes this strikes the Earth's magnetic field, causing it to shudder. When this happens we get a magnetic storm. That is just like a weather storm except that it's the Earth's magnetic field that's stormy. If we travel far enough north sometimes we can see a magnetic storm. That is what the aurora borealis (the northern lights) is.

These storms tend to get stronger every 11 years or so. This is called the sunspot cycle. When it reaches its peak, the storms can get pretty strong – so strong in fact that they knock out satellites and sensitive electronic equipment. The next one, called sunspot cycle 24, is due to peak in 2012.

It is not known exactly what causes the sunspot cycle, but some scientists believe that the planets have something to do with it. As they rotate around the sun they pull it a little off centre and some people believe that this is enough to cause some of the explosions. Indeed, in 1965 a paper published in the *Astronomical Journal* demonstrated a link between the maximum ejection of energy from the sun and its off-centre movement.

Also in 1965 a paper in the same journal showed that violent magnetic storms occurred when the planets Venus, Earth, Jupiter and Saturn were nearly in a straight line with the sun.

In 1969 NASA commissioned some research in the area because scientists were concerned about the damaging effect of magnetic storms on their satellites. This research also found that magnetic storms were particularly violent when certain planets were in alignment.

This evidence all suggests that the planets are able to affect the Earth's magnetic field. And since our nervous systems are sensitive to the field then they are actually affecting us too.

Symbols and archetypes

The second way in which the sun, moon and planets affect us, and the one that is favoured by most astrologers, is based on the idea that they all, together with the con-stellations of the zodiac (Scorpio, Taurus, and so on), have stories and myths associated with them. These stories and myths were created by the ancients and have become archetypes. Everyone knows them at an unconscious level. We do so much at an unconscious level. The unconscious mind is much more aware than the everyday mind. For instance, you don't need to consciously remember to breathe – your unconscious mind takes care of this for you. It has a finger in many pies, so to speak. It is aware of much, much more going on than we could possibly imagine. In one estimate it is believed to take in 4,000,000,000 (billion) pieces of information every second, compared with the 2,000 or so pieces that the conscious mind is able to process.

One thing your unconscious mind notices is the position of the planets and stars. Planets are moving across the sky all the time, entering constellations on the left, moving through them and popping out the other side. As a planet moves through a particular constellation, a certain story is played out. For instance, the zodiac sign Taurus is a bull and its story is that it pulls a plough across a field. In consequence it is associated with being earthy, steady and practical. The planet Mercury is regarded as the messenger of the heavens and is associated with mental ability and communication, since our mental ability aids communication. So when Mercury is in Taurus the story is that mental intelligence takes on a steady, practical tone. We all unconsciously take this story on board and tend to be more mentally cautious and practical at this time. If you were born when Mercury was in Taurus, then these traits are believed to be hardwired into your character.

It seems that the moon and the planets affect us both magnetically and through their stories. I believe the stories unconsciously influence our personalities and behaviour, while the magnetic effects are more hormonal and emotional.

Let's look at some of the evidence that shows how the planets might affect us magnetically.

The big magnet and you

Neuroscientist Michael Persinger, while head of the Neuroscience Laboratory at Laurentien University in Ontario, Canada, conducted several studies showing that the human brain is sensitive to magnetic fields. In several studies he was able to induce mystical experiences in people by applying a magnetic field to the temporal lobes of the brain.

Persinger proposed that wobbles of the Earth's magnetic field, which can be brought about by magnetic storms, could also bring about this effect. Other research has shown magnetic storms affecting brainwave EEG patterns, particularly in the frontal and central areas of the brain.

Scientists have recently found clear links between magnetic storms and depression, just as gloomy or stormy weather can cause a person to feel low or depressed.

Dr Ronald Kay, a consultant psychiatrist at the Westbank Clinic in Falkirk, Scotland, examined the records of patients admitted to the Lothian Hospital for depression between 1976 and 1986 and compared them with records of magnetic storms. When he compared hospital admissions during the first, second and third week after a storm with the same calendar months when there had been no storms, he found that there was a 9 per cent increase in admissions for males with depressed-phase manic-depressive illness in the first week, a 36 per cent increase in the second week and an 8 per cent increase after the third.

Have you ever, for no apparent reason, just felt depressed or emotionally low, and then a day, week or couple of weeks later found the feeling lifting again? Maybe there were strong magnetic storms at those times.

A 2006 scientific paper by Michael Berk, psychiatry professor at the University of Melbourne, even found a link between magnetic storms and suicide. Examining the suicide statistics for Australia between 1968 and 2002 (51,845 males and 16,327 females) and comparing with the time of magnetic storms, he found that suicides significantly increased in females during concurrent periods of magnetic storms.

Don't get scared that you are suddenly going to want to end it all when there's a magnetic storm, though. We have much more control than that. People who are already planning on suicide might just be tipped over the edge by a magnetic storm, that's all. If you're not contemplating suicide then there's little chance that a magnetic storm is going to make you do it.

The increase in depression has been linked with melatonin

levels. Many scientists have now found that magnetic storms can reduce melatonin levels in the pineal gland, which is just above the centre of the eyes. Melatonin acts as an anti-depressant and plays an important role in regulating sleep. So if its level drops, its anti-depressant effect is less and sleep might not be as good as normal.

The effects can be seen in many areas of life. In one study, conducted by the Federal Reserve Bank of Atlanta in 2003, it was found that in the week after high magnetic storm activity there was a downturn on stock returns. The magnetic storms probably affected the melatonin levels of some stock traders and corporate executives, thereby also affecting their sleep, their emotions and maybe their decision-making ability.

Magnetic storms have also been shown to affect the heart and blood pressure. In 2004 three Russian scientists discovered that blood pressure increased along with magnetic storm intensity. The stronger the storm, the more blood pressure went up.

Patients with ischaemic heart disease have also been studied for the impact of magnetic storms. In 2001 a team of scientists found that the erythrocyte sedimentation rate (ESR) of ischaemic heart patients was significantly altered during magnetic storms. The ESR rate is the speed at which red blood cells fall to the bottom of a test tube. When there is swelling and inflammation, blood proteins clump together, making the blood 'heavier' and so the cells falls to the bottom more quickly. In earlier research, the scientists found, fortunately, that they could easily shield patients with high sensitivity from the storms by creating a shielding chamber.

Other scientists, observing the possible angina-causing effects of magnetic storms, found that aspirin decreased the negative effects of the storms.

As the body of research showing how we're affected by magnetic storms is increasing, it has become clear that some people are more sensitive than others. Researchers have labelled the sensitive people 'aurora disturbance sensitive people' (ADSP). For these people, the effect of a magnetic storm might not be unlike the effect of caffeine after a strong cup of coffee, inclining them towards stress and agitation.

You can outwit magnetic storms. But you really have to concentrate, just as you would if you were pushing through a caffeine agitation or forcing yourself to sober up if you had drunk too much alcohol. Sometimes it's better to not do too much. Just sit at home and wait out the storm.

The work on magnetic storms has gone a long way towards explaining the phenomenon of geopathic stress, which is where sensitive people fall ill in certain geographical regions. Have you ever felt unwell when you moved to a new house or when you walked into a certain area? The reason for this is that Earth's magnetic field isn't uniform all over the planet. It is most intense at the poles but is also distorted in many locations by the presence of under-ground rock formations, volcanic activity and under-ground water. A map of it resembles a classic contour map showing the heights and depths of hills and valleys. So, for sensitive people, highs or lows in the Earth's magnetic field in certain geographical regions could easily make them feel a little off-colour.

Changes in the magnetic field don't always produce negative effects, however. It is just that these have been most studied. We tend to look for negative effects first. For some people, magnetic storms can be mystical and enlightening. As I mentioned earlier, Michael Persinger found that some people had mystical experiences when he stimulated their brain with magnetic fields similar to the Earth's during magnetic storms. Maybe, for some people, enlightenment is written in the stars, so to speak, just as depression or high blood pressure is for others.

Whatever the case may be, magnetic storms do affect us and we can roughly predict when there will be highs and lows by reading the 11-year sunspot cycle. And if the planets do indeed have something to do with some magnetic storms then some planetary positions really do tickle our nervous systems, affecting our hormones and our emotions.

The planets may do far more than bring on magnetic storms, of course. That is all we've studied so far because it is easy to see, but it is quite likely that planetary positions and alignments are constantly pinging the Earth's magnetic field in very subtle ways and having some very subtle hormonal and behavioural effects on people. For some the effects may be almost non-existent and for others they may be more pronounced. This probably depends on genetics, and maybe even diet and exercise level.

How animals find their way home

Animals are sensitive to the Earth's magnetic field too and many of them actually use it to orient themselves.

In 2001 scientists at Tel Aviv University tested this ability in blind mole rats. They placed one group in a maze under normal magnetic field conditions and watched where they set up home. They found that the rats moved to the southern sector of the maze. Then the scientists turned the magnetic field around so that it pointed the opposite way. When they placed another group of mole rats into the maze, they set up home in the northern sector, showing that even though they couldn't see, they were still able to find their way around by sensing the magnetic field.

Some creatures also use the magnetic field to navigate their way across vast distances. Every year, in autumn, the monarch butterfly flutters over 2,000 miles from the US and Canada to warmer weather in Mexico. For years scientists wondered how these butterflies, and in fact almost all birds that migrate to warmer climates, could make such long journeys to exactly the same place every year without getting lost. Many birds fly thousands of miles to another continent and even end up back on the same branch of the same tree in the same garden that they flew off from months earlier. Now even with a good A–Z, I get lost finding the same café I had a coffee in just a week earlier!

In 1999 scientists at the University of Kansas placed some monarch butterflies in a tabletop arena and noted that when they flew it was in a southwesterly direction, as if they were flying from the USA or Canada to Mexico. Then they masked the arena from the Earth's magnetic field so that the butterflies wouldn't feel it. This time they flew in random directions. Publishing their results in the prestigious *Proceedings of the National Academy of Sciences*, the scientists concluded that the butterflies had been using the Earth's magnetic field to head southwest.

In a similar experiment, scientists at the University of North Carolina at Chapel Hill were studying young loggerhead turtles. Just as birds fly thousands of miles and end up back on the same tree, so these turtles swim thousands and thousands of miles and end up back on the same tiny strip of beach that they were born on. They are known to migrate along the North Atlantic gyre from the east coast of the US across the Atlantic Ocean, down the coast of Spain, down the coast of Africa and then back across the ocean again and up to the US in clockwise circle. So the scientists filled a container with saltwater to simulate the ocean. Then they placed wires around the container to produce a magnetic field similar to the Earth's magnetic field. When the turtles were placed in the container they swam in a circular motion, as if they were following the gyre. They were following the magnetic field.

Because many animals use the Earth's field to keep themselves going in the right direction, they sometimes become temporarily disorientated if a magnetic storm causes it to shudder or if it has hills or valleys. Bees, for example, use a series of elaborate movements to communicate the location of nectar, but if there's a magnetic storm they make mistakes.

Some scientists have suggested that one of the reasons why whales beach themselves is because of changes in the magnetic field. By plotting the positions of mass strandings of whales onto a map showing the contours of the Earth's magnetic field, University of Cambridge scientist Margaret Klinowska found that most strandings around England occurred where magnetic 'valleys' went from the water to the shore.

In May 2004, scientists at Virginia Tech, publishing their results in the prestigious journal *Nature*, suggested that some birds could actually see the lines of the Earth's magnetic field. They proposed that the birds saw patterns of colour or light intensity superimposed upon their visual surroundings and that this was due to certain types of chemicals (known as photoreceptors and photopigments) present in the retina that were sensitive to magnetic fields. Our genetic code isn't vastly different from that of animals and we can use the Earth's magnetic field to find our way too. It is called magnetoreception. Dr Robin Baker of Manchester University in the UK blindfolded some students and drove them up to 30 miles away from the university. Then he asked them, still blindfolded, to estimate the direction of the university. They scored pretty well. When he removed their blindfolds, however, they became disoriented.

Baker then did a similar experiment with schoolchildren. They were transported in two buses and one group had bar magnets attached to their heads that would neutralize the effect of the Earth's magnetic field and the other group had magnetized pieces of metal attached to their heads. At the destination, when asked to indicate north, the group of children with the magnetized pieces of metal performed much better than the other group.

So the Earth's magnetic field affects humans and animals and is definitely affected by the sun and the moon. It is my personal belief that the small group of scientists and astronomers that link some changes in the magnetic field with the planets are correct. Therefore some planetary positions affect our nervous systems.

Planetary positions and alignments are destined, as is the position of the sun and the moon. We can calculate the position of the moon or, say, Mars from the day a person is born to the day they die with breathtaking accuracy, so at certain moments we can definitely say that their nervous system is subject to certain cosmic forces. But just as a strong cup of coffee doesn't force you to behave in a certain way, how we work within these cosmic forces is up to us. We have free will within this destiny.

How the time of birth might be destined

According to Dr Percy Seymour, principal lecturer in astronomy at the University of Plymouth, in his book *The Scientific Proof of Astrology*, the solar system is playing a 'symphony' on the magnetic field of the Earth. The biology of life hears this symphony and dances along with it. And it has been doing so for aeons.

It is likely that since the human body has evolved over aeons within regular notes played on the Earth's magnetic field (remember the 11-year sunspot cycle), it has become tuned to this symphony. This is probably why the human (and animal) nervous system is so sensitive to it.

We have seen that magnetic storms can have hormonal effects. Most research has studied melatonin, but it is likely that other hormones are affected. Women's fertility cycles, which, as we have seen, are subject to the moon, involve other hormones. Thus, magnetic storms and even subtle magnetic rhythms could, in theory, influence the timing of birth and therefore a person's astrological destiny.

I was able to find one scientific paper, published in 1998 in the *Journal of Obstetrics and Gynaecology*, which showed that the onset of labour peaked at certain times (8 p.m. and 9 a.m.). This is related to hormonal rhythms, which may be affected by the Earth's magnetic field. Who knows, but maybe these rhythms are influenced by the planets, the moon or the activity of the sun.

Michel Gauquelin used statistical methods to show that children tended to be born under the same planetary conditions as their parents. For example, if a parent had been born with a particular planet rising or near the highest point in the sky, then it was statistically likely that the child would be born with that planet in the same place.

Gauquelin found that the trend was only apparent in natural births, where the natural hormonal rhythms were intact. The correlation didn't exist if a birth was induced. He also found that if there had been a magnetic storm at the times when a particular planet was in one of those positions, the effect was even more obvious.

The human brain is sensitive to magnetic fields, as Michael Persinger discovered. Like an antenna (neural connections share some similarity to antennae), it probably detects the Earth's magnetic field and thus what the planets are up to. Percy Seymour has proposed that a foetus's brain recognizes a planetary 'signal', which is the way the Earth's magnetic field is pinged, and that this causes the release of hormones that induce the mother's labour.

A foetus shares its genetics with the mother, so it is fairly likely that it will recognize the same 'signal' as the mother. This might explain why mother and child are often born under similar planetary conditions. And, of course, it would only apply to women who were most sensitive to the Earth's magnetic field.

Michel Gauquelin found that the effect was even more obvious if the mother and father were born under similar planetary conditions. Just as both parents having the same genes for a particular part of their appearance enhances the likelihood that the child will be born with that trait, both parents' brains being tuned to the same planetary signal increases the likelihood that the child will be tuned to it too.

Destiny

The ancient Mayans were talented astronomers and had a very accurate calendar. They appear to have been aware of planetary movements and to have built their calendar around them. What is interesting is that it ends on 21 December 2012, which has been calculated to correlate with a rare alignment of planets and is also when the sun and the planets line up with the centre of our galaxy for the first time in 26,000 years. Furthermore, sunspot cycle

24 is also estimated to peak in 2012 and is expected to yield the strongest magnetic storms for a long time. So perhaps we will all experience some hormonal and behavioural effects at that time.

There have been prophecies that 2012 heralds the end of the world as we know it. Indeed, there is a link between sunspot activity and our weather. Part of the global warming phenomenon, for instance, seems to be related to sunspot activity, although the overwhelming cause is our choice to burn fossil fuels at an alarming rate.

Perhaps, since magnetic storms can induce mystical experiences, 21 December 2012 will herald a time of spiritual enlightenment. If so, then we can expect many changes to the way the systems of the world operate.

Maybe the symbolic ending of one great cycle and the beginning of another will resonate deeply in our unconscious minds and truly herald the beginning of a new age.

The Seven-Year Itch

A study published in the *Journal of Personality and Social Psychology* showed that even when we're not aware of certain words that we read, we still take in their meaning and are influenced by them. In one experiment, scientists from New York University gave 30 undergraduate students 30 sets of 5 words that they were told were to measure language proficiency. Their task was to construct a sentence containing 4 of the 5 words from each set.

This was a so-called priming experiment and the scientists were attempting to prime some of the students with words associated with the elderly. They had interspersed the words 'old', 'lonely', 'grey', 'bingo' and 'wrinkle' in several of the sets.

At the end of each student's turn, the scientists pointed

them towards the lift down the corridor. Unknown to the students, one of the experimenters was sitting in the corridor with a hidden stopwatch and timing how long it took each student to walk the 10 yards from the experiment room to a piece of silver carpet tape on the floor.

Students who hadn't been given words associated with elderly people took on average 7.30 seconds to walk the distance, but those who had been given the 'old' words took on average 8.28 seconds. That's 13.4 per cent longer. Just by reading words that were associated with age, the students had begun to walk more slowly, just as elderly people would.

In another priming experiment published in the same journal in 1998, scientists at Nijmegen University in Holland found that associations could affect a person's performance in a game of Trivial Pursuit.

In one experiment, the scientists had a group of students imagine what a typical professor was like, including how they would behave, their lifestyle and physical appearance. They had another group of students do the same for a secretary. After answering 42 Trivial Pursuit questions, the students who had been primed with the stereotype of a professor scored 59.5 per cent correct answers compared to 46.4 per cent for those who had been primed with the secretary stereotype.

In another experiment the scientists compared a group

thinking of a professor with one thinking of a football hooligan. Those thinking of a typical professor scored 55.6 per cent correct answers compared to 42.5 per cent for the students thinking about a football hooligan.

Of course, this had nothing to do with the real abilities of professors, secretaries or football hooligans, but it showed each participant's *unconscious* view of how that stereotype would perform.

So, dear readers, I wonder what kind of priming conversations you might strike up the next time you play a game of Trivial Pursuit? I know that I'll be asking my opponents what they think of Neanderthal man.

Our stories

In a similar way, we all have stories about ourselves that influence what happens in our lives. For instance, if your story were that you were intelligent, you would almost certainly do better at Trivial Pursuit than if your story were that you weren't.

But our stories are about much more than intelligence. Many of us see ourselves as the hero or heroine of our lives, the person who wins through against all the odds, the person everything happens to, the lucky person, the unlucky person, the healer, the wounded healer or the eternal victim. There are many others, too, but if you ask people, most of them don't realize that they have even one of these stories going on. It's all happening unconsciously. Even though we may not realize we have these stories, they influence how we act in our lives and even shape what happens to us. Say that I had the story of achieving against all the odds going on. Without even realizing it, I would describe my day to you as if I were the main character in that story. Say I had just started a new job in an office. Later that evening, telling my friends all about my first day, I would probably say that it was a good job but that there was a mountain to climb to master it, there were sooooo many challenges and the boss gave me loads of stuff to do, but (of course) I got through it all, although I had to stay till six to get it done. Regardless of what else happened that day, that is what I would remember most and be motivated to talk about. I would view my day – and my life – through 'against the odds'-coloured spectacles, so to speak.

Also, without even being aware of it, we will seek out opportunities to be the main character in our stories. If I had the hero story going on, for instance, I would probably attract opportunities to be the hero in my daily life – thereby missing opportunities to be someone else – and so my life would begin to follow the direction that my story was taking it in. This is how the stories we have shape our lives.

We align ourselves with the stories of our astrological signs too. Most people have a rough idea of what the signs are like from reading their 'stars' in newspapers and magazines.

Some, without even thinking, will begin to behave in the way appropriate to their character.

Superstitions

Superstitions are also stories that we align with. Do you know that more people are admitted to Accident and Emergency departments due to traffic accidents on Friday 13th than at any other time of the year? A doctor once pointed this out to me.

In a paper published in the *British Medical Journal* in 1993 a team of scientists showed that even though there were far fewer vehicles on the M25 motorway around London on that day (presumably many superstitious people stay at home), admissions to hospital from traffic accidents were 52 per cent higher than on Friday 6th.

Conducting a much wider study, a team of scientists from the University of Oulu in Finland, publishing in the *American Journal of Psychiatry* in 2002, compared the deaths from traffic accidents on Friday 13th in a national population with deaths from traffic accidents on other Fridays of the year. They found that more people died in traffic accidents on Friday 13th than on any other Friday. Interestingly, the increase was mostly in women (maybe they're more superstitious) and 38 per cent of deaths involving women on Friday 13th were a direct result of Friday 13th itself. There was no difference in female deaths on any other Friday, but a large peak on Friday 13th.

The authors believed that this might have been due to the anxiety of the Friday 13th superstition, something known as paraskevidekatriaphobia (bet you can't say that!), which comes from the Greek.

So the effects of Friday 13th are not due to some dark force that makes us crash our cars, but to fear itself. It's our belief that Friday 13th is 'unlucky for some' that causes accidents. It's all in the mind.

This doesn't mean we should dismiss it, however. The placebo effect is also all in the mind and we can't dismiss that. The effects of Friday 13th are real for some people, just as surely as the placebo effect is real and the resulting chemical changes in the body are real. But the advantage of it being all in the mind is that you can free yourself from it just as surely as you can change your mind.

We all know the stories...

As I mentioned briefly in the last chapter, the planets and the constellations of the zodiac have stories associated with them. Steady and dependable Taurus the bull pulls a plough over a field, while Libra is depicted as the scales and therefore represents balance and hence fairness, justice and diplomacy.

The planets have stories too, or rather personalities. For instance, as I mentioned earlier, Mercury is the messenger in Roman mythology and represents communication. Jupiter, being the biggest planet, represents growth and expansion, both physically and intellectually. Jupiter was the Roman king of the gods, while Venus was the Roman goddess of love and so the planet Venus represents 'feminine' qualities like love and empathy.

When a planet finds itself moving through a particular constellation, its personality is coloured by the story of the constellation. For instance, if Venus is in Libra, its loving quality is coloured by fairness, justice and diplomacy. Therefore a person born when Venus is in Libra might often find themselves sympathetically listening to others' problems.

A person's birth chart shows the positions of all of the planets in relation to the constellations of the zodiac at the moment when they were born. It is therefore a map showing the type of stories that are likely to be in that person's unconscious mind throughout their life. The skill of an astrologer is in the interpretation of the stories that they see in a chart.

As we saw earlier, the unconscious mind takes in much, much more information than the conscious mind. Even though we don't tend to know consciously about the myths and stories associated with the planets and the constellations, and where they were in the sky when we were born, unconsciously we certainly will. If seeing words associated with the elderly can make a person walk more slowly and Friday 13th can result in more traffic accidents, then it is fairly likely that the stories in our chart will be played out, to some extent, in our lives.

The myths and stories are stereotypes, although they are more commonly referred to in astrology as 'archetypes'. At the unconscious level, everyone knows about them. So just as the stereotype of a professor caused people to perform better at Trivial Pursuit, so the archetypes of the planets, their personalities and the constellations influence our behaviour too.

Jung described a 'collective unconscious' connecting us all. I like to think of it as being like the Internet. Think of yourself and everyone else as a personal computer and imagine that we are all connected via the Internet. All of the content of the Internet – or the collective unconscious – is available to any of us. At an unconscious level, we all share knowledge and information. In this way, even if a person hasn't learned anything consciously about stereo-types, or archetypes, they will still have the information to hand and it can still influence their behaviour.

I sometimes like to refer to our connection as being like a u-net, to draw the comparison with the Internet, with 'u' meaning 'unconscious'. And just as you can send e-mail via the Internet, so our thoughts are like u-mails.

People pick up on our thoughts, emotions and intentions at deep unconscious levels.

In an experiment conducted at Bastyr University in Seattle in 2003, for instance, researchers placed a person (the receiver) inside an fMRI brain scanner. Another person (the sender) viewed a flickering light in another room. While the light was flickering in front of the sender, the fMRI scanner focusing on the receiver picked up an increase in activity in the visual cortex of their brain. Even though it was the sender who was viewing the light, the receiver's brain was also acknowledging it. The sender had sent a u-mail and the receiver had picked it up. (In my first book, *It's The Thought That Counts*, there are examples of similar scientific studies.)

Comets and eclipses

Comets and eclipses are also examples of stories we tell ourselves. When we see them in the sky our unconscious minds recall stories of omens of disaster, or at least they used to. Disasters happened during the appearance of some prominent comets centuries ago and so for many years the association between comets and disaster was etched into the collective unconscious. Take Halley's comet, for instance. One of its appearances coincided with the Battle of Hastings in AD 1066, so people made the association.

However, with the advent of more powerful telescopes at affordable prices which have enabled more people to take up astronomy as a hobby, many more comets are being discovered and I believe that this drowns out the omen/disaster association that we used to have. Every comet that is not associated with a disaster reduces the power of the stereotype. It would be the same with a game of Trivial Pursuit if the people thinking about secretaries kept on winning. Any people watching who thought about secretaries in the future would associate them with intelligence.

It's the same with eclipses. The power of TV and the Internet means that there is much more talk of eclipses now than there was in olden times. So now they are associated with daily life rather than sudden disaster. In the science of NLP (neuro-linguistic programming), which many people are familiar with, this process is known as 'collapsing an anchor'.

The planets and DNA

It is well known that mental and emotional states activate some of our genes. Stress, for instance, produces stress hormones in the body. Therefore any powerful story, or even symbol, will have genetic effects.

The swastika is a symbol that might well produce a strong reaction and thus activate a number of genes. Prior to the rise of German National Socialism, it was actually an auspicious Hindu symbol meaning 'It is well.' However, since its adoption by the Nazi party its meaning has been completely changed in the collective unconscious. To almost everyone it now produces a feeling of fear, stress or revulsion.

The Om symbol is another that is likely to activate certain genes, this time ones that produce calming hormones for the body. This is a Hindu symbol representing God, the manifest and unmanifest, and the entire universe.

The stories that are played out by the planets are likely to have genetic effects too, because of how they make us feel.

Cycles and the seven-year itch

As well as astrological signs, portents and stories, we are also influenced by astrological cycles. Some astrologers believe that major aspects of our lives change every seven years or so, a period of time linked with the movement of both the moon and Saturn. Both move approximately a quarter of the way around a person's chart every seven years. Uranus is also linked with the cycle of seven. It takes 84 years to move around the sun and this is thought of as 12 seven-year periods.

Many people link these seven-year changes with relationships – these tend to either break up or grow stronger at these times. Often children are born then. Other people experience career changes every seven years. Some just find that something significant happens in their life at seven-year intervals.

According to these cycles, changes generally occur at ages 7, 14, 21, 28, 35, 42, 49, 56, etc. They are even associated with biological rhythms. Adolescence usually comes at about the age of 14, for instance, while adulthood is thought of as the age of 21. When a person reaches 28, they tend to be challenged to step into their true selves. Some move into a career that is set to be theirs for life. The age of 35 can herald an acceleration of this. Many people make large career jumps then, to director or vice president of an organization, for instance. Spiritually, people can make large jumps of consciousness at this time. Buddha is said to have achieved nirvana at age 35.

Another significant milestone is 42, which is halfway around the 84-year cycle of Uranus. This is the age of the classic 'mid-life crisis', where a person comes to see their life in a different way. To the unconscious mind, the cycle is halfway through and so people see one phase of life ending and a new one beginning.

Of course, the planets don't force these changes upon us. It is our unconscious awareness of the cycles that influences our behaviour and how deeply these archetypes resonate with us as individuals.

Personally speaking, I began having my first spiritual thoughts at approximately age seven. I went through puberty around the age of 14. When I was 21, another significant change occurred – I finished my honours degree and began my PhD.

About a month after my 28th birthday I had a moment of tremendous inspiration and clarity with regard to my life. I made the decision that I would leave my job in the pharmaceutical industry within the next year and move back to Scotland to be near my family. It was a day that changed my life. It was the clearest that I had been about anything for a long time.

I was offered a publishing deal for my first book, *It's The Thought That Counts*, a month short of seven years after my momentous decision. And this was seven days short of my 35th birthday. I'm 36 at the time of writing this, so I'll let you know what happens when I'm 42.

Of course, these cycles are just approximate and not absolute. They do not affect everyone to the same extent, just as not everyone is magnetically sensitive and not everyone reacts to pharmaceutical drugs in the same way. But you'll be surprised just how many people's lives follow approximate seven-year cycles. And if you look closely, you might even see the beginning of a change about halfway through the cycle.

There are longer and shorter cycles, too, corresponding to the movements of other planets. Mercury takes 88 days to rotate around the sun, for instance, and Mars takes about two years.

The magnetic effects of the sun and the planets affect us in cycles as well. Every 11 years or so the sunspot cycle peaks and therefore magnetic storms peak too. So for sensitive people, melatonin levels in the pineal gland (third eye) will be reduced every 11 years. It is likely that the resulting emotional effects will cause some people to behave differently and perhaps bring about changes in their lives.

Certain planetary alignments come in cycles too. As they line up, the Earth's magnetic field gets a 'ping' and so does the human nervous system. Our DNA has evolved alongside this magnetically rhythmic sound – developing to the tune of the cosmos. Therefore I believe that we are genetically predisposed to recognize certain magnetic cosmic signals.

One very obvious genetic response to the cosmos is found in a gene known as zif-268, which switches on during the sleep cycle when we are dreaming. It produces a growth factor that promotes the growth of the brain and it aids the remembrance of dreams. Night occurs due to the rotation of the Earth on its axis. So this rotation, a cosmic rhythm, is related to the switching-on of zif-268. Basically, zif-268 responds to a cosmic cycle.

Melatonin is also produced at night-time, to regulate our sleep–wake cycles. This is why we get jetlag when we travel, because the melatonin rhythm is upset. This rhythm is also related to the cosmic day–night cycle.

Magnetic fields similar in intensity to those during magnetic storms have also been found to have genetic effects. Russian scientists exposed rats to artificial magnetic fields similar to the Earth's magnetic field during a magnetic storm and found that their offspring were less active than other rats and committed more errors in lab maze tests.

Ultimately, how much can the planets affect us? It probably varies from one individual to the next and most likely depends on the planetary positions at the time of birth, the stories that these represent, the person's magnetic sensitivity, the genes that they inherited from their parents, their diet and exercise, and even how much astrology they know.

But even with sensitive individuals, free will can still overrule these cosmic forces. Despite their effects, statistically not everyone is affected, so obviously we are not at their mercy. We have the capacity to override them. Cosmic forces seem to act like gentle winds that blow our canoe left and right, but free will is a paddle that we can use to steer in any direction we wish. The sun, the moon, the planets and the stars can incline a person's life in a particular direction, but free will can set its own direction.

DNA - *Nature* *via* Nurture

We are born with genes that determine our appearance, our health, our intelligence and our behaviour. How fixed is this genetic inheritance? Does it leave any room for free will?

You are what your great great grandparents ate

Over 30,000 people died of starvation during a famine in Holland between 1944 and 1945. But for those who survived, the legacy of the hunger carried over to succeeding generations. Years later, a group of researchers who were investigating the effects of the famine found that the children of some mothers that survived were born with a lower than average birth weight. Going further, some of the grandchildren had lower birth weights too.

A publication in the journal *Heart* in 2000 also found an 8.8 per cent higher incidence of coronary heart disease in people born to mothers who experienced the famine.

Other researchers found that if a man experienced famine prior to puberty then his grandchildren tended to have a lower risk of diabetes. This study also showed that if the man had overindulged during that period then the risk of diabetes in his grandchildren was four times higher.

On or off

Most of us are born with the same genes. There is a 99.9 per cent similarity in genetic code across the entire human race. Many of the differences that emerge in life are down to whether the genes are on or off.

Human DNA has about 25,000 genes, so imagine DNA as being like a long cable, like the cable attached to the plug on your TV set, but lined with thousands and thousands of tiny light bulbs. The bulbs are flashing on and off in patterns, just like the way Christmas tree lights flash. But instead of thinking of the lights as being on or off, now imagine that each has a dimmer switch, so that not only can it be on or off but it can also be bright or dim.

Research has shown that genes go on and off and become bright and dim in response to what we eat, how much exercise we take and also how we feel. Our life experiences create the dimmer switches that can turn the brightness up or down or, in genetic terms, affect the activity of a gene.

Recent research in a field of science called epigenetics has even revealed that the effects of an intense or long-term experience are passed on to our children. It's as if the switch has been pressed so many times that it has got stuck.

For instance, say your mother had genes that gave her deep blue eyes, just like her mother and her mother before that, but through some ingredient in her diet her eyes turned pale blue. After that, even if you inherited the genes for dark blue eyes that had been in your family for generations, your eyes might be pale blue too, just like your mother's. Even though you inherited the dark blue eye gene, you inherited the consequences of your mother's diet too.

A 2007 paper in the *Journal of Neuroscience* even found that a rat mother's care of its young could alter the activity of genes that controlled the brain's response to stress. If a rat pup had been cared for, when it grew into an adult it was less fearful and more confident. Further studies revealed that these epigenetic changes were passed to future generations. It is likely that the same occurs in humans.

Therefore, as well as passing on your genes to your children, you pass on your life experiences. Essentially, your genes have memory. And research has shown that this memory is passed down several generations.

In 2006 scientists at the Centre for Reproductive Biology at Washington State University found that if rat embryos were exposed to specific environmental toxins that caused specific diseases then the diseases (prostate disease, kidney disease, immune system abnormalities, testis abnormalities and breast cancer development) were passed on for four generations.

Similarly, scientists studying the fruit fly *Drosophila melanogaster* found that when a particular gene called Hsp90 was overactive it produced mutations in the fly (protrusions from its eye) that persisted for a further 10 generations.

If this effect is representative of genetic behaviour in humans then your health today might be coloured by what happened to your great, great, great, great, great, great, great, great grandparents.

So if a great grandparent experienced famine and the result was a dimmer switch that turned down the brightness of some healthy genes, you might have that dimmer switch today and be experiencing the effects of the famine too. And it's not just famine. Scientists have shown that any sustained experience can create a genetic dimmer switch. This could be famine, overeating, sustained joy, sustained physical activity or even a long bout of sexual activity.

So what we do now can affect our children's health, and their children's health, and that of several generations down the line. Part of our children's destiny is coloured by what we do today and part of our own destiny is coloured by what our ancestors did.

But this doesn't mean that our children are at the mercy of this 'health destiny' or that we are at the mercy of our ancestry. Research has shown that we can neutralize these effects through free will.

For instance, scientists at Duke University, publishing in *Molecular and Cellular Biology* in 2003, reported that the offspring of mice born with an abnormal gene (agouti gene) that made them yellow and extremely obese were born normal if the mother was given a nutritionally rich diet. So even if you inherited a particular switch, your choice to eat well could be the deciding factor in how things turned out for you and your children.

Similarly, if you have been born into a family with a history of, say, heart disease or cancer, this doesn't automatically mean that you will develop it too. It's up to you. It will depend on how you lead your life. Choosing to exercise regularly and manage your stress levels could play a large part in your future health.

Applying this to physical and mental abilities, it also means that even if your family hasn't featured anyone good at sports or academically distinguished, you could still become a talented sportsperson or gain a PhD. Research has shown that our hopes and dreams, as well as our life experiences, switch our genes on and off, and the brain and body develop accordingly.

Destiny is not written in our genes. They only serve as a template. We get to paint the picture of our own life.

Outwitting our genes

Genes don't simply switch on and off at random. They do it in response to their environment. If you think of the light bulbs as little musical bulbs that play their note when you touch them, then our habits, diets, lifestyles, thoughts and emotions play tunes on our DNA. The song of your life is whatever you choose it to be.

For instance, a person with 'average intelligence genes' might grow up to be exceptionally intelligent if exposed to the right parents, teachers and coaches. The brain of a child is highly 'plastic'. Its growth is easily influenced by its circumstances. A person with 'genius genes', on the other hand, might not distinguish themselves intellectually if they grow up in an environment that isn't productive for them.

And, as I mentioned, even if none of your family has been good at sports, you still have the potential to be a champion athlete. Literature and films are full of stories of people who have achieved greatness against all the odds (although I'm not suggesting you take on that story). Others might be born with a genetic edge over you in terms of size and strength, but sheer determination more than compensates in most cases. History has shown us that it's really down to what you want and how much you want it. Free will overrules genetics.

Indeed, recent groundbreaking scientific studies have even shown that enriching life experiences and physical exercise can promote brain cell growth (neurogenesis) in adults, something that was thought to be impossible only a few years ago.

When something enriching, exciting, stimulating, fascinating or joyful happens to us, we consciously replay it over and over in our mind with emotional intensity. As we do so, this constructs the memory at a cellular level in our brain. Genes switch on because of the emotional intensity of the event and they build up parts of the brain. The biological 'size' of the memory – how many neural connections and brain cells are made – depends on how much the event meant to us on a mental and emotional level.

It even happens in our sleep. Studies have shown that if a day has been full of memorable experiences then during REM sleep genes switch on that construct proteins and brain cells.

If you imagine yourself doing something so intensely that you feel you are really there then the brain and body will grow to your pictures. The brain doesn't know the difference between something actually happening to you and you just imagining it happening. If you can dream it, to the brain you're actually doing it.

If it's perfect health that you're visualizing, then you will influence your body in a healthy way. If it is being more intelligent, then your brain and body will grow in the right way for intelligence. And if it is being good at sports, then your brain and body will mirror your athletic dreams.

In preparing for the 1980 Winter Olympics, the Soviet squad was divided up into four groups. The first group was to do their usual physical training. The second group was to do 75 per cent of their usual training and spend 25 per cent of their training time visualizing themselves performing. The third group was to do 50 per cent of their usual training and 50 per cent mental work. Group four was to do 25 per cent of their training as usual but spend 75 per cent of the total training time doing mental work. At the Olympics, group four's performance was most improved, followed by group three, followed by group two, followed by group one.

The extent of the mind's influence over the body can be seen in studies of people with multiple personality disorder, which is usually a consequence of a severe childhood trauma that literally shatters the personality into fragments. Each personality develops its own view of the world, its own beliefs, its own likes and dislikes, and even its own talents. When a person switches personality, which involves a mental and emotional shift in who they believe themselves to be, their biology rapidly shifts too. Studies on brainwave patterns have shown that when a personality switches, the brainwave patterns change. In addition, muscle tone, heart rate, handwriting style, artistic talents, posture and even visual acuity and shape and curvature of the eye also change. In one well-known example, one personality was allergic to orange juice and would come out in hives when they drank it. But when the personality switched, the itching immediately stopped and the water blisters began to disappear.

What this shows is that the mind has the capacity to overrule the body. The placebo effect also shows this. In one study on the placebo effect, students who were known to be allergic to poison ivy were blindfolded and rubbed with a leaf. They were told it was poison ivy and as a result they came out in a rash, but it was really a maple leaf. It was their belief that had caused the rash. Another group was told that they were being rubbed with a maple leaf but it really was poison ivy. This group didn't come out in a rash, though. Their belief had overpowered their normal allergic reaction.

The mind has far more ability to overpower the body's programming than most people think. I have heard many people say that the reason they are easily stressed is genetic – their mother or father was highly strung, so they can't help it. It may be that they have inherited a tendency to get stressed easily, but this doesn't mean that they are destined to be stressed for life.

Say you work in a high-pressure environment. You might be in a sales job, for instance, and feel the pressure of striving to make sales. Your genes might mean that you are more inclined to react to the stress than other people are. But you are not destined to be stressed out for the rest of your life.

If you think about it, it's not actually the job that's causing the stress, it's how you are dealing with the job. It's what you are telling yourself that you need to do (your story). And that is causing biochemical chaos in your body. As well as producing the adrenaline that puts you on edge, the genes that produce stress chemicals compromise the immune system, the heart, the liver and the kidneys.

But you could use free will to adopt a different story. You could tell yourself, for instance, 'My health is more important than my job' or 'It'll get done eventually.' That way your genetic tendency to get stressed could be overruled by your new story. You could also practise meditation to improve the way you deal with the pressured environment. That would prevent the suppression of your immune system and any damage to your organs. So even if you were born with a tendency to get stressed, you could outwit your genetics and have stress-free days, even under the most testing of circumstances.

We are born into a biological destiny that is determined by the genes of our parents and further compounded by their life experiences – what they ate, how much exercise they got, the traumatic or enlightening events that happened to them, how they felt – and also by the experiences of *their* parents, and theirs before them.

But research has shown that our life is not completely genetically predestined. We can switch our genes on and off, and as they respond to what we do, what we have inherited takes a back seat. The deciding factor is how we act, what we eat, how we exercise and how we think and feel *now*. Through exercising our free will we can change our genetic destiny.

Life before Life

- Preincarnation

Evidence from people who have had near-death experiences (NDEs) and from people under hypnotic regression suggests that life goes on after we die. Furthermore, it points towards life before birth as well. One of the most intriguing findings to come out of this research is that we actually appear to choose aspects of the life we are about to live. If this is so, then the life we are born into is not a blank canvas ready for us to sketch out our lives, but many of the features, landscape and people are there already and the events are lined up waiting to happen. Let's look at some of the research into preincarnation and the choices we make there.

Near-death experiences

A near-death experience is where a person is brought back from the brink of death but remembers what happened to them while they were being resuscitated and the ECG was flatlining.

These experiences are more common than you'd think. Millions of people around the world have had them. In a Gallup poll during the eighties, for instance, around 1 in 20 Americans reported that they had had one.

A landmark study by cardiologist Pim van Lommel that was published in 2001 in the prestigious medical journal *The Lancet* followed 344 consecutive cardiac patients who had been successfully resuscitated following a cardiac arrest. The research team found that 62 of them (18 per cent) had had a near-death experience.

There are various degrees of NDE, ranging from leaving the body and watching the resuscitation procedure to going into a light and coming out on the 'other side'.

One woman told me of an experience that her mother had had as a 10-year-old child. She said she could:

> '...*vividly describe the [hospital] procedure – what she saw, what was going on and what she heard. She described the tubes and the red blood going into a jar and the people in the room. She said she was watching it up on the ceiling, out of her body. She seemed quite calm, just observing it all.*'

Looking down on a scene like this is called veridical perception. Another woman told me it had happened to her mother too:

> *'She was a young woman undergoing a major operation to remove a piece of bone from her hip to replace the bone that had become diseased on her spine. She had had TB in the lung when she was 14 years old and although she did recuperate, it reappeared a few years later and was eroding the bones in her spine. It was the first operation of its kind in Scotland [1954/5]. The nerve pain was excruciating. During this long procedure she said that she was suddenly aware that she was floating above the operating table and could overhear the conversation below. She had no pain and was aware of a light. She felt drawn to the light and was not unduly concerned that she had apparently left her body. Then she was aware of coming around after the operation.'*

Some people actually go into the light and pass through a tunnel before appearing on the other side. Here they are usually met by relatives and loved ones who died years ago. Many NDEers also report being met by an intelligent light source. This often turns out to be an angel or a religious figure like Christ, Buddha, Krishna or Muhammad.

Some people's experiences are even deeper. They have a life review where they watch every detail of the life they have just lived unfold in front of them. They say it's like being in a large 3-D cinema and seeing panoramic images of their lives played out as if they were really there again. And the most amazing part of this life review is that you feel the impact of everything you ever thought, said or did to the people around you. If you caused someone pain, for instance, you feel the pain, and the pain that person went on to cause another, and the pain they in turn caused someone else. And where you showed love, you feel the love and how that propagated too.

The point, NDEers tell us, is to emphasize that thoughts, words and actions have consequences, even when we don't immediately see them. And the most important part of the review is to show us how powerful love can be. In fact, the point of life is love.

An NDE almost always changes the person who has it. In van Lommel's study, patients were interviewed after their resuscitation, then again after two years and after eight years. For most, it had a lasting positive effect. They tended to show their feelings more, to be more accepting of others, to be more loving and empathic, to have a greater involvement in family life, to have a greater sense of the meaning of life, a greater interest in spirituality and a greater appreciation of ordinary things. They also had much less fear of death and a greater belief in the afterlife.

In the book *Home with God* Neale Donald Walsch describes an additional stage that some NDEers experience. He describes a merging with God, or the equivalent in other religious or spiritual traditions, an experience of total oneness with all life, a state of absolute and indescribable bliss where all pain dissolves away and all that is left is the core of your being. He claims that this is what happens to us all eventually.

A new paradigm in science

This is hard to accept in the scientific community. The traditional view of consciousness is that it is a product of chemicals in the brain, so it exists only when the brain is alive. Once the brain 'flatlines', there can be no conscious experiences.

But I believe that we are on the brink of a major break-through in our understanding of consciousness. I believe we will come to accept that it is independent of the body.

With the advent of powerful new brain imaging tech-niques, our understanding of the brain is already beginning to shift. We are learning that some of what happens in the brain is *caused* by what we're thinking about. It's not just a one-way street where chemicals produce thoughts and emotions.

For example, fMRI brain imaging shows that some areas of the brain light up when we think of a certain thing. In February 2007 a research team's discoveries in this field made media headlines around the world, as did their view that in the future it might be possible to read people's thoughts by working out which areas of the brain matched which thoughts. This research clearly showed that thoughts affected the physical matter of the brain.

The old belief was that consciousness was created by the brain. The emerging view is that consciousness is independent of the brain and the body.

In fact there has never been any definitive proof that the brain creates consciousness. Prodding parts of the brain has been shown to affect consciousness, so the assumption has been that consciousness must be housed in the brain. But new theories suggest that the brain is more like a radio antenna that picks up the signals of consciousness. If the antenna is poked or prodded then of course the signal will be distorted.

When the brain dies, consciousness is no longer 'received' by the brain and the five senses, so it is able to perceive things outside the body. This is how many NDEers are able to watch over their resuscitation procedures.

Dr Michael Sabom, an NDE researcher, once did an experiment involving 32 people who had had NDEs. He asked them to describe the resuscitation procedure that was performed on them. All of them reported it accurately, with no major errors. He also asked 25 quite medically knowledgeable people to describe the resuscitation process, but 23 of them made major errors in their descriptions. The people who had had NDEs really had been watching from above.

Dr Brian Weiss, a well-known and respected psychiatrist practising in Miami, Florida, has performed hypnotic regressions on hundreds of his patients as a therapeutic technique. In one regression, which led to the writing of the excellent international bestseller *Many Lives, Many Masters*, a patient actually went back to previous lifetimes and the space in between lives. Since then many of Weiss's patients have described the same events as NDEers. Some of them have also reported the experience of choosing the next life. Apparently we not only experience a life review when we die but also a life preview before we are born.

What we choose and why we choose it

The life preview is where we select the conditions that we would like for our next lifetime. We choose our parents and the social and economic situation that we will be born into. We choose to have certain skills, talents and abilities. We even choose our physical appearance.

You may wonder why we would choose these things, but if you have ever taught, been a coach or trained people in any way then it will make total sense to you. I used to be a long-jump/triple-jump coach. In one training session I might have restricted the distance the athletes were allowed to run prior to jumping. This would have taught them to accelerate quickly, to focus their minds on the jump and to know that they could jump a long way no matter how fast they were moving. On another day, I might have placed a ramp at the beginning of the sand. Jumping off it would have given the athletes more height and being in the air longer would have allowed them more time to master the technique. All the conditions I created for the athletes were set up so that they could develop their jumping ability.

Likewise, the conditions we choose before birth (preincarnation) enable us to develop our abilities. This is what NDEers have told us, what hypnotized patients have told us and what spiritual teachers have been telling us for thousands of years. Our choices set out the training conditions within which we develop. This is why life can be hard at times. As a coach, if I hadn't set challenging conditions for the athletes, their progress would have been limited. And working under the same conditions every time wouldn't have enabled them to develop.

Some people like to think of life as like a play. We are the characters, and the costumes and scenery are how we set the stage before making our entrance. If you think of life as a play, it is one that involves improvisation. There is a script, but it is only a draft. In life, it would do little good if you followed a script word for word. There's no development opportunity in that. You need space to express yourself creatively. That's when growth occurs.

NDEers tell us that one of the main things we work on in life is emotional development. Say your plan for this life involved working on compassion. You would then select the conditions that would give you the best chance of developing it. So you might find yourself around people who were in pain, for instance, so that compassion was able to stir in you when you saw them suffer.

But it's not just emotions we work on. We also choose to develop our ability to alter the reality around us, or to stretch the limits of human mental and physical potential, or even to work on our sixth sense and the abilities that relate to it. The circumstances that we are born into set the perfect conditions for whatever it is we have chosen to do. But it's up to us how we work things through.

Destiny

Imagine your life as a river. It starts with your birth as a melting crystal of snow high on a mountain and ends when you reach the sea. During the life preview, you set out the flow of the river. The conditions you choose at birth – your physical and mental capabilities, your preferences, parents, social and economic environment, even physical location – set the initial direction.

Further down the river, you arrange with other people (as per their life preview) to meet and form relationships that will help all of you to fulfil your goals. And you might also set up some obstacles and challenges that will help you to develop. Having placed the obstacles up ahead, it is easy to assume that those aspects of your life are predestined. But destiny is not as set in stone as you might think.

It is a very wide river that you're born into and there is a lot of room for moving left and right and forwards and backwards, which means that you can avoid the people and events that you have planned to meet if you want to. Your exact course isn't definite. You could just as easily hug the left bank, or the right one, as go right down the centre. You could even go under the water at times or find yourself floating on air.

Many of us do have a sense of destiny. This feeling comes from the fact that we are born with a deep unconscious memory of our life preview. So we have a sense of the course of the river, where we are heading and even whom we're heading towards. That's why many of us just know what we're supposed to be doing, even though we can't explain it. And why we can meet people for the first time and feel as though we've known them all our life.

This sense of destiny is like having a tiny map in your mind that guides you along the river. It's an inner knowing of where you're going and what you need to do. Everyone has it, although some of us are more conscious of it than others. It's the memory map that puts you on autopilot sometimes. Then you find yourself just doing something without thinking. At other times it prods you to move to a different career, to move to a new place and even to 'recognize' people along the way and form bonds with them.

But you always have free will. The map doesn't force you to do anything. It's just a guide, just as a street map is a guide. A street map doesn't force you to go down a particular street. It might make it obvious which would be the best route, but it doesn't force it upon you. And it is the same with the internal map. It might cause you to have a feeling about something or someone, to have an instinct about which choice to make or to feel inspired about what to do or where to go. It might even give you a clear picture about what you need to do, but the choice is always yours.

For example, you might have agreed with the soul of your potential husband or wife that you would meet, fall in love and get married at a certain time, and this will be clearly marked on both your maps. It will even be written in the stars. You will find each other, no matter where you are. Even if you were born in different parts of the world, the unconscious attraction between the two of you will see you both guided to the same place at the same time, as if pulled through space and time by an invisible magnetic force. Looking back, you might be amazed at all the things that had to happen to enable you to meet – all the coincidences, even the role some people played in it all. And when you do meet, there is an instant attraction. It's a recognition, or more accurately a remembrance. Somehow, deep down, you remember each other.

Of course, it doesn't always happen this way. Some people choose to do it differently, because doing it differently will better serve your spiritual goals. Your maps might indicate that you should be friends for a while or even hate each other at first. But whatever way it happens, you can bank on it being just the perfect way for both of you.

A pull towards a person often has an element of destiny, then. There's always a good chance that we're going to end up with that person for a while. Chances are that we'll fall in love, especially if there are children involved, who will have their maps ready and waiting for us to get together.

But free will is involved in how you get to the meeting with the other person and what state you arrive in. Although there will be a high probability of the meeting happening, there will be many paths leading to it. And even when you meet this 'soul' mate, it is still up to you whether you actually start up a relationship or not. Destiny is not set in stone. You can lead a horse to water, as they say, but you cannot make it drink.

It's all in the timing

When we have our life preview, not only do we choose a particular place in which to be born, but we also choose a particular time. Nothing is random. This is so that the planets, which are destined to be in certain places at certain times, can influence us in ways that complement our chosen path.

It would do little good, for instance, if our map had us making a radical change at, say, the age of 42, or making a change that led to a meeting with a soul mate, when astrologically this would be a bad time for us. The stories carved out by the planets might not be right for such a change at that time and there might be magnetic influences that wouldn't work for us either. By looking at the whole map before we are born we can time certain changes – twists and turns on the map – to coincide with the behaviour of the cosmos.

We also build triggers into our genes. Remember, the map is psychological – it's a memory/imprint – and thoughts and emotions can trigger genes to switch on and off. So your memory of the life you wanted can result in genes switching on at specific, perfectly timed moments of your life, when you unconsciously recognize that you've reached a certain part of the map. It may be that a sudden inspiration activates the genes and all of a sudden you have an incredible longing to be a writer, or artist, or actor, or teacher, or researcher, or parent, and with the right genes activated you now have the ability to be it.

To make sure all this works, the timing and location of birth have to be pretty exact. Just 10 minutes difference or a few hundred miles east or west can give a completely different astrological chart. Ask any astrologer! In other words, when a soul decides it's time to be born it will come, and not a moment sooner.

Whispers from the other side

If you exist on the 'other side' before you are born and after you die, it doesn't take much of a stretch of the imagination to assume that there are other 'people' – spirits, beings, angels – there too. NDEers tell us there are and opinion polls show that the vast majority of people believe in their existence.

In the book *Destiny of Souls*, counselling psychologist Dr Michael Newton relates the hypnotic regressions of many of his patients and they describe, with astonishing similarity, the nature of the 'other side' and the reality of 'life' for the souls who live there.

There is no definitive scientific proof of this in that we can't physically measure anything. And to the average scientific mind it probably sounds preposterous. But how can we know? All we're left with is what we ultimately believe, what feels right to us individually.

I personally believe that we have spirit guides and that deceased relatives sometimes visit us. About 20 years ago both my mum's deceased parents visited her, one night after the other. My gran, who had died a few years earlier, looked as real as a person. My papa, who came the next night, looked more like a photographic negative. He was semi-transparent.

I once went to a seminar by psychic medium Gordon Smith, whose accuracy in relaying information from people's deceased relatives was absolutely astounding. One girl's brother 'came through' and Gordon suddenly found himself humming a tune, and then his hands and arms started to move in a rap movement. It turned out that the song was the 'dead' brother's favourite song. It was a rap song.

Gordon has actually been scientifically investigated. Professor Archie Roy, Emeritus Professor of Astronomy at Glasgow University, wrote, 'Gordon Smith provides names, addresses, events and descriptions sharply relevant to a person's life and the lives of those they have known.'

Of course it's unlikely that deceased relatives, spirit guides and angels just sit around on clouds all day waiting to communicate with us. Heaven is not a physical place where we hang around for eternity. As Pope John Paul II pointed out, it is a state of mind. Deepak Chopra, in his excellent book *Life After Death: The Burden of Proof*, makes the point very clearly that we continue to develop on the other side.

Sometimes this development can be achieved through service to people still on this side. This, presumably, is the role played by spirit guides. They help us throughout our lives, infusing our minds with thoughts and ideas that help us to make the right choices and to get out of sticky situations.

So, as well as having an unconscious memory of our life map, we are reminded of our hopes and dreams by our spirit guides, and probably also by deceased relatives. I have always felt that my papa is watching over me. Although it might sound daft to the scientific mind, I find comfort in communicating with him in my mind. And I believe that he helps me when I ask. Sometimes I get a clear picture in my mind or a feeling or an inspiration about something. I believe this is his way of impressing the answers upon me.

Spirit guides do the same thing. Some mediums get even clearer messages, perhaps hearing a voice or physically seeing their guides and having conversations with them. It's also very common for people to see deceased loved ones a day or two before their own death. Many nurses have seen them too, although few publicly admit it.

Sometimes, even if we don't hear our guides that well and screw things up a bit, so to speak, they are always there to help us pick up the pieces and get started again. And, who knows, maybe the 'screwing up' was all part of the plan and there is an opportunity for growth amidst the ruins. That might have been the whole point.

For instance, say you wanted golf to be a sport that would provide the ideal playing ground for your evolution, but that through some reckless behaviour you ended up damaging your shoulder so much that you could no longer swing a club. This would by no means be the end of your chance for development. All that would change, really, would be the landscape in which you evolved.

Every situation provides development opportunities. When I was a coach, for example, I could have suddenly changed the training session and added or removed obstacles. I could even have handicapped the athletes by adding weights to their legs or arms. But whatever I chose to do, the opportunity to develop was always there. All that changed was the immediate environment and the conditions the athletes had to work in.

Going back to the golf, maybe the injury was all part of the plan. Golf was only right for you up to a point, so your inner compass guided you to indulge in the reckless behaviour that resulted in the injury. Everything happens for a reason, even if we don't always understand what that reason is. Usually an abrupt end to one thing is part of the plan that opens the door to another.

Look, therefore, not so much for what you can get out of life, but how you can adapt to a changing environment. Change is inevitable. It is the only thing in life that doesn't change! If something doesn't go to plan, don't be quick to assume that it's a disaster. The seeds of your development may lie amidst what you think of as ruins.

Your spirit guide is likely to draw your attention to this in some way. You may overhear people talking about a similar issue, you might find it in a book, you may hear it in a song or you may 'just know' it and not know how. Your guide will then assist you in making choices that create the next set of circumstances that are ideal for your development.

Knowing what's ahead

Sometimes whispers from our guides alert us to what lies ahead. At other times getting a sense of things ahead of time could be just recalling a future bit of our map. I mean, we did see the whole map before birth, so we must 'remember' at some level what's around the corner. Sometimes glimpsing the future might be a bit of both. You might sense a point up ahead on the map and your guide might say, 'Yes! That would be a good thing. And if it doesn't happen now, it will later.'

I can give you an example from my own life. When I was a teenager and during my studies at university, every now and then I felt a spontaneous wave of enthusiasm at the thought of understanding the nature of reality and how the mind interacted with it, and teaching it and writing books about it. And just so you know how unrealistic this was at that time, it took me two attempts to pass my English exam at high school. On my first attempt I was 22nd out of 22 in the class during a prelim exam. Later, during my PhD, I handed in such a poorly written report that my professor, William J. Kerr, organized for me to go on a six-week writing course that was set at a basic high-school level.

After my PhD, I went to work as a scientist in the pharmaceutical industry and worked in the drug development process for three years. Every now and then I still felt waves of enthusiasm and excitement about writing 'my' book, but what I was doing seemed a million miles away from it. I mean, I was working in drug development and I wanted to write a book about metaphysics and the power of the mind – how on earth did I think I was going to do that?

It was during my fourth year in the industry that things began to change. In 1998 I was offered a job managing changes in the company. I had only been in the new job for about six months when I had the huge inspiration I wrote about earlier. In my heart, that changed everything for me.

That realization took place during the Christmas holiday period and when I returned to work in the new year, I became fidgety. About six months later I was on a Tony Robbins 'Unleash the Power Within' seminar. There I had my biggest surge of inspiration, excitement, enthusiasm and clarity so far – testimony to the quality of Tony's workshop guidance – and became totally committed to resigning from my job and moving back to Scotland. I was going to give talks and run workshops about the power of the mind to create what you want in life and to heal yourself from illness. And of course I was going to write a book.

My first attempts at writing weren't that good, however, and I lost all my savings trying to promote myself as a speaker. Although I knew in my heart what I wanted to do, I lacked confidence. I wanted to speak, but I was terrified of it. Thirteen people turned up for my first workshop, nine of whom were family and friends who wanted to support me. Three of the others were people I had met the week before when I was out with friends. They had agreed to come along if they didn't have to pay. Only one person had actually responded to my eight weeks of advertising at £140 a week.

Finally, between 2000 and 2002, I did start writing my book. But I threw it away about three or four times. Looking back, I can see that I wasn't ready to write at that time. When I was ready I started again and didn't stop until I had finished.

So it doesn't matter how outrageous your idea is. If the thought of it makes your heart sing then maybe it is meant for you. Maybe it's your destiny, what you chose during the life preview, and your spirit guides are now whispering in your ear, planting thoughts in your mind and tickling your heart so that you feel great every time you imagine the possibility.

Everything happens in its own time, though. Although I was receiving inspirations about writing 15 years before I actually wrote a book, I didn't do it until I was ready. If you are receiving inspirations about something now, maybe the time is now, but don't panic if you don't have the courage to follow your heart right away. Maybe it's not your time yet. Maybe it won't be your time for another 25 years or so. Have patience and enjoy your life in the meantime.

Spiritual evolution

Hypnotic regression and spiritual traditions tell us that we have lived many lives. Each time we die, after a period of assessing that life, we choose our next life and continue our spiritual evolution. In *Destiny of Souls*, Michael Newton's regressed patients gave precise details of this.

Think back to my coaching example. Once an athlete had learned all he could from me he could choose to move on to another coach, maybe even one in a different town. That would be like a new life for him. His new coach, recognizing his new level, would set him new challenges. Through this new 'life' he would be able to take his skills even further. He might even go on to become a champion.

After that, another phase of his life might begin. He might find a partner and have children. His challenges then would be very different from his early training sessions with me, but they would enable him to grow and mature in a new way. Each new phase of his life would offer new opportunities for development.

It's a bit like this over many lifetimes. There's so much to master, it just can't be done in one span of 80 or so years. Spiritual traditions call it the reincarnation cycle. We may go through it thousands of times.

Scientific evidence of this has come mainly from studies of children, who seem to retain memories of previous lives much better than adults do. Once they reach about five or six years old, the memories fade away. In many reports young children have recalled past lives in incredibly accurate detail. When meeting their past families, they recognize them instantly. When travelling to their past homes, they know how to get around the area perfectly. In their mind, it's only been a little while since they were last there.

As we go through the reincarnation cycle we have countless experiences, growing more mature as we experience more intricate emotions, hone our skills and master our ability to attract the things we want in life.

Take peace, for instance. In one lifetime you might have learned that you can feel at peace by sitting quietly and listening to the sound of your breathing. You might have become really good at it. But you want to become even better. You know that you have the potential to take peace much further than this. You reckon you could find peace amid much more challenging circumstances. So you might choose to be born into a large family where there is always a lot of noise or be drawn to friends whose behaviour is chaotic. In these situations, finding time to sit still isn't quite so easy. You are so challenged that you need to learn to be extra focused to be able to find peace. You have to learn some new tricks, which might also be part of the plan. The old way isn't going to work this time. You have to stretch yourself.

With this in mind, practise looking at your life situations not as burdens, which we all do at times, but as opportunities to take yourself to new heights. Personally, I thought that I was good at being peaceful. That was until I took a job as a college lecturer while I was writing my first book. With one class of 16-year-old boys, it was so challenging that when it was over I sat in my car and cried. Within the first 10 minutes, all of my peace and positive thinking had gone right out of the window. But I later reminded myself that as well as having a chance to make a real difference to their lives, I had an opportunity to develop myself.

By the end of the course I felt like Robin Williams's character in the film *Dead Poets Society*. I had a queue of 16-year-old boys waiting to shake my hand. Some said they felt that they had learned more on that 12-week course than in all their school years. And I had learned a lot too. I had grown in confidence and I was much more relaxed. In terms of my personal growth, that was probably the whole point. Teaching that class was probably on my map both for my own development and so that I could do some good in the lives of those boys. And it was only by stepping out of the reality that was facing me and looking at it from a spiritual perspective that those breakthroughs were possible.

It was painful at first. But having painful experiences is important for our development. We don't become experienced by reading books and going to talks. We become experienced when we apply what we've learned to our life situations. We grow more when we actually do it.

It doesn't always work out, of course. But if you don't master what you set out to do in one life, you can try again in another or move on to something completely different if you want. It's always up to you. At the end of your life you'll go through the life review and learn from it. Then you'll make some changes that will make the conditions better for you to master whatever it was you were aiming to do, perhaps making it a wee bit easier this time so the experience is less intense. You might do this again and again and again, under varying conditions, in various times and places, until you do master it.

The end point is when there's nothing more that physical life can challenge you with. You are whole, complete. Nothing can faze you. You see everything for what it really is. Your whole existence is to teach and serve. This is the state achieved by all great masters.

The Science of the Soul

In *Destiny of Souls*, Michael Newton's patients revealed that when we are born only a part of us experiences physical life. The biggest part of us stays at home, on the 'other side'. It's as if the part that is born is the tip of an iceberg. The biggest part of the iceberg stays under the water, or on the other side. That is your soul. So you are part of your soul, experiencing life in a particular way and evolving through countless lifetimes.

Your soul experiences physical life through you. It's like dipping your finger into warm water. You feel it, but it's the finger that has the actual experience. If it had consciousness, it might tell its friends how the water felt, and it might experience happiness or sadness depending on whether the water was to its satisfaction or not. And because the finger is a part of you, you know how the water feels too and you feel the finger's joy and pain.

The ocean current

The river that is the journey of your life is really, really wide. In fact, to extend the metaphor, imagine that it's not a river at all. Imagine that it's an ocean. Therefore you are born into an ocean current that flows in the direction of the choice that you made before birth.

As you go through life you drift in the direction that the current takes you. And as you flow along with it you work on the qualities that you choose to work on – maybe compassion or forgiveness or peace. The current takes you to events and people that will help you develop these qualities.

But because you have free will you are not confined to that exact current. You can change your mind.

Your internal map will inspire you to make the choices that help you stay with the original current. But it's always up to you whether you want to listen to that inner voice and do anything about it. Being born into a predestined current but having the free will to change it means that the forces of destiny are in balance with the power of free will.

Sometimes you have to do the work

Every thought, idea or dream that you have sets new currents. That is the power of free will. The more you think a thought, the stronger the current. Much of the time your thoughts are in harmony with your map, so your free will creates your destiny. You have an instinct as to where you're supposed to be going, so your thoughts create the right currents that get you there. Sometimes, though, your thoughts are about things that are not on your map. Through your free will, you create currents leading there too.

Some events on your map are very important for your development and they have a high degree of destiny to them. These things often just happen. They can hit you like a thunderbolt, right out of the blue. But sometimes the goal that you set yourself before birth was to learn that you have the power to create your own experiences in life. In that case, you need to make certain key events happen, otherwise they might not happen at all. The point with this is that you learn a) that your thoughts create your reality and b) how to create what you want.

This is something that many of us are learning in our current lifetime. How does it work? Through sometimes painful situations as well as joyous experiences you come to realize that your thoughts attract both the good and the bad. You gain experience of intentionally thinking about certain things and noticing that you attract them like a magnet. Your map and your guides inspire you with dreams and you have to use this magnetic power to make those dreams happen. It's as simple as just holding the thought in your mind to the exclusion of all other thoughts. By focusing on what you want instead of complaining that you don't have it, or worrying about the future, you learn to attract the things you want and to live out your dreams.

What can stop us realizing our hopes and dreams are disbelief and fear, especially if our dreams are far removed from the kind of life we are living right now. When we don't believe that we can live a dream, our thoughts drift to what will happen if we don't get there, what the consequences will be, what difficulties we might face and a host of other dire possibilities. We even think of lesser dreams and aim for them instead. So we create currents tugging us in all of these directions.

The net effect of this is that you don't go anywhere fast. Sometimes you think about your dream and other times you worry about it. You are being pulled in several directions. Eventually the strongest thought, or current, wins.

If the dream is strong in you, you will eventually make it happen, however, because many currents will be taking you to the same place, regardless of how far away it seems. But it might take a lot longer than you hoped.

So, when you have a dream that inspires you, trust that what's happening now is part of the plan, regardless of how different your life is from what you want it to be. When I was a scientist, my dream to write books about love, the power of the mind and metaphysics seemed a million miles away, but being a scientist was actually the perfect route for me to take. It enabled me to develop a scientific way of looking at things, I was able to access and understand scientific journals, and my credentials made it easier to get my voice heard and my writing taken seriously. So if you have a dream, trust that you're supposed to live it out. That's why it inspires you. Don't imagine that you couldn't possibly have it.

Don't worry about how it will happen, either. Have you ever been told just to 'let go' or 'surrender'? When we do this, we drop our concern about how things will turn out. But we don't drop the dream.

Quite often people get themselves to such a level of pain that they say, 'That's it, I don't care any more.' Funnily enough, it's only then that things begin to work out for them. It's a paradox for most people because they think that to get what they want they need to not want it.

When a person gives up like this, what's really happening is that they are stopping worrying about how things will turn out. And when the fear leaves, the dream has a chance to work. The person's focus moves away from the worry of it not working out, leaving the current to flow *towards* it.

You don't need to reach such a level of pain that you 'don't care any more'. You can still want something and not be overly concerned about it. Letting go, or surrendering, is the same as trusting that whatever is happening right now is just right for you.

Of course sometimes your dream isn't right for you and you were never meant to live it, but it was meant to be part of your route to something that was even better for you. I mentioned earlier the example of having a golf dream but getting injured so you couldn't pursue it. The whole point is your development. Therefore everything that happens – whether you live your dream or not – is always for the best.

Let this be your mantra: 'Whatever happens is for the best.' I have used it a lot in my life. I can shoot for the stars and if I don't get there then I know that that wasn't the best thing for me at that time.

Your soul does it all

Your soul is part of an even bigger soul, which is vast. Some call it an oversoul. It experiences all of the currents in the ocean. Think of it as being like a guitar string. If you pluck the string, it will vibrate and appear to take the shape of a bow. This is your eye seeing the string in hundreds of different positions. The start and the end point of the string stay the same, but there are many paths that the string can take to get from one end to the other. Your oversoul will explore all of them. It will experience every vibration, so to speak. These will be currents running parallel to your own.

With the guitar string, if you were to take a snapshot with a camera, you would see the string in only one position.

But all the others exist too. If you were to take another snapshot you might see a different string position. It already existed before you took the snapshot – you just hadn't seen it then.

Similarly, each time you follow a different current in the ocean it will be new to you, but it already exists and your oversoul is already exploring it. Your consciousness merely gets into phase, or flow, with it.

It's a bit like a child's computer game. The computer knows how to respond to any move that the character makes because every conceivable move has been pre-programmed onto the disc. It would be wrong to say that only one possible path through, say, a jungle game existed, because every possible move is on the disc.

So as we flow along with our current, every move that we could possibly make has been pre-programmed, so to speak. But this doesn't mean that our choices are pre-destined. We can choose any of the pre-programmed 'moves' using our free will, just as you can go left, right, forwards, backwards and jump at any time in the computer game. The moves are not limited, so free will is not limited. Of course, there are still some events (moves) that are more probable than others, because they are part of your memory map, but you always get to choose.

The ocean contains a field of infinite possibilities where we can make infinite choices to go to infinite destinations.

We are limited only by the mental limits we impose upon our dreams – whether we believe they are possible or not. And your oversoul is the ocean that contains all of the possibilities that you might come to know. Its desire is for you to be anything you want to be.

What does your oversoul get out of all this?

This is in some ways the ultimate question. What is the reason behind it all? Is there a purpose to it? Why is your oversoul doing it?

The answer is that your oversoul evolves through the experiences of its children – and you are one of its children. Think of your own parents for a moment. They experience joy for every joyful moment you feel. They enjoy success when you enjoy success. They feel happy when you feel happy. They are still free to pursue their own goals, but much of their time is spent in service to you. They dedicate themselves to you so that you can be all that you dream of being. In a similar way, your oversoul is in service to you. Service is one of the qualities that it is working on. It gives itself to you for your happiness and growth. It is dedicated to you.

And just as you grow from a child into an adult, so you yourself grow into an oversoul over many, many lifetimes. Only it's a wee bit different in that your oversoul exists outside time and space. So you literally grow 'out of this world'. And when you become the oversoul you realize that you were in service to yourself all along.

This might sound paradoxical. How can you be serving yourself now if you're not due to be able to do it yet? Have you gone back in time? But this is the reality, and the science, of the soul.

Imagine there's a whirlpool ahead of you representing your final destination. It's a very special whirlpool, one that you cannot possibly conceive of at the moment. When you reach it and enter its centre, you will realize how special it is. It's a whirlpool that causes you to merge with the entire ocean. It's an infinity whirlpool. When you enter it, you become infinite and know all there is to know. You become an oversoul. And as the entire ocean, you can immediately be anywhere you want to be. You can be at the start of a current (that is, at the start of a life), in the middle or at the end, and you can even be in all those places at the same time. In this way, as an oversoul, you can be of service to yourself before you become an oversoul, as bizarre as that sounds. You only need to imagine a point on a particular current and you will be there.

It's a bit like getting to such a level of technological advancement that you are able to build a machine that lets you go back in time. Except we're not talking about technological advancement here, but spiritual advancement. With your time machine you might wish to travel back to help the child that you once were to get through a tricky time. Imagine that the time machine puts you out of phase a little, so that you are invisible to your past self, but you can still offer it guidance. Only its conscious mind cannot hear you. So the child feels your guidance as inspirations, instincts and gut feelings. You could help it to understand that everything will turn out OK, thus lessening its fears. It will then tackle situations with an inner knowing that everything will be OK. In this way your soul, which is your distant future self, continuously walks beside you and advises you.

This time-travel metaphor is not quite as far out as you might think. Many indigenous cultures believe that we travel through time in our dreams. You can do it at any time in your mind – you only have to think of a past time and you're there. But your oversoul really is there. It's not bound by the same laws as you are.

Or the laws you think you are bound by... Modern scientific studies have actually shown that our minds can go back in time and change things, as outrageous as that may seem. There have been a number of studies, many conducted at Princeton University by the Princeton Engineering Anomalies Research (PEAR) group, where people could view a stream of random numbers and by thinking of one number could make it appear more than any other. Taking these experiments further, some researchers recorded a series of numbers and then played them for the participants a few months later without telling them that they had been pre-recorded. To the participants, this was just another experiment where they had to influence the numbers. And they did. The 'outrageous' hypothesis, as one scientific study put it, that resulted was that the human mind was capable of going back in time and, as long as no one knew what the recorded numbers were (they were sealed), was able to change the past just as easily as it could change the present.

Maybe we do this all the time. I don't think there's any way of knowing. But these studies do point towards the reality of an oversoul. That reality is strange to us now and defies our rules of time and space. But once we reach the level of the oversoul, it's just the way it is.

Let us return to the time-travelling metaphor. Suppose you go back in time and offer your past self different advice so that it chooses a different current from the one you have chosen. In the reality of the oversoul, these two possible currents exist side by side, just like two positions of a guitar string – the one you remember having and the one your past self is 'now' exploring. And, being the oversoul, you experience both of them, just as you would experience both hot and cold if you were to dip one finger in hot water and another finger in cold water.

Ultimately, all currents lead to the infinity whirlpool where you dissolve completely into the ocean and know all of it, all at once. Mystics have told us that we can experience this at any time. Many people, in fact, have had momentous glimpses of it. In some cases it changed them forever and set the rest of their life along a spiritual path. Many people who have had an NDE have caught such a glimpse.

So, to recap, what your oversoul gets out of your life experiences is the joy of helping you to have what you dream of. As a coach, I developed through the help I gave to the athletes in my squad. In a similar way, your oversoul evolves through the love and service it provides for you. Never be afraid to ask it for help or think you're being a burden. Being asked to help an athlete was, for me, always a privilege, never a burden. For your oversoul, helping you is the greatest joy it can experience.

Karma and changing the future

In his hypnotic regressions Dr Brian Weiss occasionally took his patients into the future, which he called hypnotic progression. One of the things he found out about the future, which he revealed in his book *Same Soul, Many Bodies*, was that it is not fixed. The future changes all the time, depending on what you are doing now. So not only does what you do now affect what happens in ten minutes' time, but it also affects your next life.

Some people believe that in the next life we have to pay for our sins. But it doesn't work quite like that. Your next life is affected by what you do now because if you accomplish what you want to in this life then you'll naturally want to move onto something else in the future. And if you don't, then you'll probably want to try again. It's just like accomplishing things in your daily life – like scoring a basket in a game of basketball, for instance. If you couldn't do it, you'd keep trying until you netted it. Maybe you'd move a little closer to the basket to make it a little easier each time. And once you had accomplished it then you'd want to move on to something else. Maybe you'd want to make it a little more challenging or to try a different game.

So if, for instance, you came into this life to work on forgiveness but didn't fully master what you had hoped – you bit off slightly more that you were able to chew – you might choose to work on forgiveness again in the next one. You might choose different circumstances, different skills and different aspirations that would enable you to really 'get' forgiveness this time around. You might even enter a different time period. Viewing it from the present, under hypnosis in the psychiatrist's chair, if you were to peer into the future, you might see yourself being bullied in the next life, or being abused in some way, or even being ignored or disrespected. But this would not be some karmic revenge or punishment for not having been forgiving enough this time around. It would be so that you could learn to forgive the perpetrators. It would be your choice in order to develop.

There is no external force that sees you punished or having to pay for your misdemeanours. All forces come from within you, just as the influence of Friday 13th is an inner one and the power of the stars lies in your unconscious reading of their stories. You may be hurt in the next lifetime, but only if you believe it will help you to grow.

Karma is a pull towards balance. It doesn't leave you without choice. It is a manifestation of your intelligence – the intelligence that understands that to know something completely you need to see it from both sides.

And greater awareness will change the future. If, armed with the insight from your hypnotic progression, you found it in your heart to genuinely forgive the people who had harmed you or your loved ones in this life, another session in the psychiatrist's chair would almost certainly reveal a completely different future lifetime. You would have no need to repeat the forgiveness lesson next time around.

Ultimately, being the entire ocean, your oversoul experiences both the current where you forgave in this life and the current where you didn't, and it contains the destiny(ation) of both those currents. Ultimately, they are the same – the infinite whirlpool.

What does science say about all this?

Scientists believe that the material world is made up of what is known as the quantum field. It is an ocean of energetic vibrations that small particles like quarks, protons, electrons and their friends condense out of. Mystics agree, but they say that the field, or ocean, is alive – an ocean of consciousness, pure intelligence. They say that it is God.

All things are made up of protons and their friends, and so all things, including you and me, condensed out of the ocean of consciousness. We condensed out of God and are therefore parts of God.

I have referred to the ocean as the oversoul. God is a much bigger ocean. Your soul is part of your oversoul, which is a part of God.

Science also describes the oneness of life, most notably in the theories of David Bohm, Professor of Theoretical Physics at Birkbeck College, London. He imagined the entire universe as a single living organism – an undivided whole. Although he didn't believe that it was consciousness itself, he did succeed in showing how everything was part of it.

In the book *Wholeness and the Implicate Order*, Bohm described what he called 'implicate' and 'explicate' order. Implicate order is the ultimate reality, the hidden reality underneath what we see the world to be. In other words, what you see when you look around you is only the tip of the iceberg. The real business is going on underneath. In effect it's saying that beneath the quantum field there's something else, a place that everything comes out of. Explicate order is the everyday reality that we see when we look around us.

I believe that the hidden reality is the reality of the over-soul. Its dreams are our outer reality.

David Bohm used the analogy of a hologram to explain that the hidden reality was 'enfolded' into everything. Just as you can look at any part of a hologram and see the whole image, Bohm suggested that every part of life contained the whole.

Bohm's implicate order is similar to how the mystics describe God, or the infinite field of consciousness. God exists in every atom. You can find Him everywhere. This is what is meant by Christ's words, 'The kingdom of God is within you and all around you. Lift a stone and I am there; break a stick and I am there.'

In quantum physics there is also a theory called the 'Many Worlds Interpretation of Quantum Theory'. According to this theory, an infinite number of parallel universes exist, just as an infinite number of currents exist in the ocean, to use my example, or an infinite number of guitar-string positions exist.

Scientists arrived at this theory by studying the behaviour of tiny particles as they were fired from a laser towards two slits. They found that under some conditions an individual particle appeared to go through both slits at the same time. Their conclusion was that two worlds existed at the quantum level. In one world the particle went through the slit on the left and in another world the particle went through the slit on the right.

Taking it into the real world, Nobel Prize-winning physicist Erwin Schrödinger described his now famous 'Schrödinger's Cat' thought experiment. In it, a cat sits in a box alongside a lethal poison. As long as the lid remains closed we can't know whether the cat is alive or dead. The Many Worlds theory states that it is both alive *and* dead. According to the theory, two parallel worlds exist. In one the cat is alive and in the other it is dead. When we lift the lid off the box we can only know one of those worlds. To us, the cat will either be alive or dead. This is why we can only experience one current in the ocean at a time. But the oversoul of the cat will have the experience of having died in the box and of having stayed alive, just as your oversoul experiences all the possible currents in the ocean.

Many paths exist in life. Your oversoul experiences all of them, but you experience the one that you choose, the one that reflects your thoughts and your actions.

The future, therefore, is not set in stone. You create it as you go along. Your internal map guides you towards people and experiences that will help you to develop, but you don't always need to say 'yes' to them. The forces of destiny are in balance with the power of free will.

Life isn't quite a blank canvas. Background, landmarks and people are sketched in to guide you, but nevertheless you have unlimited potential to paint any picture you wish.

And what you do create serves as a springboard for the next life, so that you can continue your development where you left off.

In the next chapter I'll describe how to unleash the full power of your free will to attract what you want in this life so that you can make the most of both the present and the future.

The Law of Attraction

Have you ever thought about a person and then they phoned you or bumped into you on the street? Have you ever visualized something you wanted and then been introduced to someone with just the right connections to make it happen? These are very common occurrences.

The phone one has been scientifically verified. In a scientific study led by biologist Rupert Sheldrake, whose research is funded by Trinity College, Cambridge, four people were selected to make a telephone call to a person and that person had to guess which of the four it was. Chance says that they should have got it right one out of four times. But in this experiment the participants got it right almost one in two times. Their success rate should have been 25 per cent, but it was 45 per cent. The odds of this being chance are a trillion to one.

If you asked someone for help, they'd probably oblige. At least they would where I was brought up. Bearing in mind that we are all connected at the level of the collective unconscious, it isn't too much of a stretch of the imagination to consider that maybe when we want help, people unconsciously pick up on our request. If this is so then they may, without even thinking about it, be drawn to us, and we to them.

Evidence that our thoughts can be picked up by other people is accumulating. One experiment that shows this is where a person sends thoughts (usually pictures) to a person who is asleep. The theory is that the sleeping person will pick the thoughts and pictures up in their dreams. In 2003, after analysing 47 separate dream experiments that involved 1,270 individual trials, psychologists Simon Sherwood and Chris Roe of University College, Northampton found that the overall accuracy in receiving a picture was 59.1 per cent. According to chance, it should have been 50 per cent. The fact that so many experiments were analysed in this case provided conclusive statistical proof that a person's thoughts could be detected by another person while that person was dreaming. The odds of this being chance were calculated at an astronomical 22 billion to 1.

So it is highly likely that your intense thoughts – your hopes, goals and aspirations – find their way into people's dreams while they sleep. And I believe that the people most likely to pick up on your goals are those with whom you share an emotional bond, although people that you have never even met will pick up on them too, especially if they are featured on your internal map and it's your 'destiny' to meet them. In fact you know them from the other side, so you do already share an emotional bond.

Earlier I described a scientific experiment where an fMRI scanner showed a receiver's brain lighting up when a sender viewed a flickering light. In this experiment an emotionally close couple was used. With random couples it wasn't as successful, as you might expect. I have always believed that I'm more sensitive to the mental and emotional states of people I'm close to than to those of random people. Haven't you? But I believe, at some level, that everyone picks up on everyone else's thoughts. It just seems to be stronger with people we're close to.

Indeed, in a similar experiment conducted at Edinburgh University in 2004 with 26 couples, 10 randomly paired strangers and 5 people who weren't matched with anyone but thought they were (therefore they unknowingly did the experiment alone, to serve as a control), a correlation was found in the EEG rhythms between the senders and receivers. The researchers found a match between the couples, as you would expect, but they also found a connection between the non-related people, although no change in the electrical activity of the brain was found with the unmatched people.

Similarly, at the Institute of Noetic Sciences in 2004,

senior scientist Dean Radin and some of his colleagues tested 13 sets of friends who were not emotionally bonded as couples but who shared an interest in the study. One person in each pair was connected to an EEG machine with a closed-circuit TV camera pointed at them. The other sat in front of a TV screen in another room and was also connected to an EEG machine. At randomly timed intervals the sender's TV screen flashed up a live image of the receiver's face.

The EEG machine connected to the sender showed a peak, as you might imagine, with the sudden appearance of their friend's face on the screen, but the receiver's EEG also showed a peak. In other words, in mirroring the fMRI results, the receiver's brain thought it was seeing an image, even though it was the sender who saw it.

Dean Radin reported the above studies in his excellent book *Entangled Minds*. I would recommend it to anyone seeking scientific proof of our interconnectedness.

I like to use the metaphor of a spider's web to describe the way our thoughts radiate outwards and people feel them. How does a spider know that a fly is stuck in its web? It feels the vibrations. In a similar way, people feel the vibrations of your thoughts. Those emotionally closest to you, or with whom you have an emotional charge, feel the vibrations more strongly. But everyone feels them, even if they just amount to tiny ripples, because we are all part of the collective unconscious.

When you strongly imagine having a dream come true, the pictures in your imagination send vibrations outwards throughout the web and then people who can play a key role in that dream begin to gravitate towards you, just as they would if you were to call for help. The way you are brought together is worked out by your unconscious minds.

Attraction in action

The law of attraction has this unconscious communication at its root. It is the law that says you attract what you focus on. Every day, we attract people and situations that reflect what we are focusing upon, although most of the time we don't even notice it because we're not aware of the law.

I often write in coffee shops. I enjoy the atmosphere and usually get good work done there. In December 2005 I went to a local town called Stirling, in central Scotland, intending to set up my laptop in a coffee shop called Costa. I arrived at about noon and went to the bank to use the cash machine as I only had a small amount of change in my pocket. I put my card in the machine but it got swallowed up. I sighed at the thought of having lost my card and then did a really daft thing: I took out my other card and put it into the same machine. Of course that was swallowed up as well.

Now I was stranded in Stirling with only £1.87 in my pocket, which wasn't even enough for the bus fare home.

And after a quick phone call I learned that I couldn't get picked up for another five hours.

The money was only enough to buy a cup of coffee from Costa and I figured that I'd need to buy a coffee to justify setting up my laptop and using their power supply. I was hungry, but I didn't have enough money to get any lunch. Knowing about the law of attraction, I quickly realized that there would be no point crying over spilt milk, as they say. If I focused on negative things like not being able to get any lunch and that my bank cards were now lost and getting replacements delivered would be a hassle, then I'd only attract more misfortune. In fact I could pretty much bank on things getting worse. So I played a wee game of mental gymnastics and convinced myself that this was a good thing. I could treat the not eating as a meditation, or even a fast. I had recently read about the positive health effects of fasting once a week. I thought it might make me clearer in the head too. I often get a wee bit drowsy after lunch. And if I had been able to get money I would have bought an almond croissant along with my coffee. They are quite sugary and I had been eating quite a lot of them recently. So not eating one would be good for my health. I was feeling better now. I was much more positive.

When I arrived at Costa I got my coffee, took a seat at a table in the corner and set up my laptop. Guess what I was writing about? Yes, how our thoughts attract. I was a few minutes into my coffee when a woman sat down at the next table along from me with a coffee and an almond croissant. As I was so hungry, it smelled even more appetizing than usual. I almost started salivating. It would have been easy to complain that I couldn't afford one and to ponder on my misfortune, but I didn't. Instead, I just imagined how great it would be to be eating an almond croissant right now.

It must have been three or four minutes later that the manager of the shop, a man called Lee, came over and handed me a plate with a croissant plus a little pot of butter and a little pot of jam and said, 'On the house!'

I had been writing in Costa, on and off, for almost two years and this had never happened before. It was the law of attraction in action. My desire had vibrated the web and Lee had felt it and suddenly been inspired to offer me a croissant. OK, it wasn't an almond croissant. But it actually worked out better because, as I said, I had been eating a lot of sugary almond croissants recently. The plain one was healthier.

The story doesn't end there. Shortly after enjoying the croissant (minus the jam), I was writing that everything was interconnected. A thought came to me that I should phone my bank in Glasgow, 25 miles away, and report my lost card. I had a direct line number for my bank manager, Maria, so I rang her.

The phone rang out for a while and I was just about to hang up when someone picked it up. It was a lady called

Christine. She sympathized with me while I explained what had happened and told me that the same thing had happened to her a month earlier. Like me, it was the first time she had ever lost her card in a cash machine. She had been in a town called Stirling... I stopped her there. 'What a coincidence,' I pointed out.

It got even spookier, because it turned out that she had lost her card in exactly the same machine.

The power of belief

So if we are all interconnected and we attract what we focus on, why don't our dreams come true?

One of the reasons is that we lack the belief that they can. With a negative outlook like this, we send out vibrations along the strands of the web that attract the circumstances of our dreams not coming true. So we might find people who agree that it's not possible. We might attract people who once had a dream and it didn't work out for them. We might even attract a situation that pushes our goal even further away.

For instance, say your goal was to open your own restaurant one day, but you had been looking at your finances and thinking that you'd never raise the money. Now, by the law of attraction, someone you'd cooked for recently might tell you they had had a bad reaction to your food.

Something might go wrong with your car and it might turn out to be very expensive to get it fixed. And then you might get a bill from the taxman that was much higher than you'd thought it would be. All of these things would seem to push you even further away from your dream. But if you were to examine your thoughts, you would find that what was happening around you was just a mirror of what was occupying your mind.

On another day, if you were feeling really upbeat about your idea, you might attract people who would tell you how much they loved your food and would ask if you'd ever thought of opening a restaurant. And then you might get a couple of unexpected cheques in the post. But again, what was happening to you would just be a reflection of what you were focusing on.

Another side to our thoughts attracting what we focus on is that they influence our behaviour unconsciously. It's as if you upload your dream into the u-net that I described in Chapter 2, in the same way that you might upload a web page to the Internet, and then you 'download' information in the form of intuition and inspiration, just as you download information from the Internet. And just as seeing the words 'old' and 'grey' can make you walk more slowly, so you'll find yourself taking a different route to work, or feel an impulse to say something, or find an idea just popping into your mind. That's because you downloaded the instructions.

For instance, when you're dwelling on thoughts of not having much money you might unconsciously drive your car harder – unconsciously bouncing over every bump on the road and skimming them in just the perfect way to cause maximum costly damage to your car.

Or, when you're complaining that you're really late for work, your unconscious mind might see a nail on the road and guide you right over it. Bang! You have a puncture, so you have fulfilled your dream of being late. It *was* what you were focusing on. You attracted what you focused on. You created the reality of being late.

Miracles – a deeper side to the law of attraction

Modern mind-body science has shown us that our thoughts and emotions are linked to our body. They can cause measurable biological changes. And just as the law of attraction attracts people and circumstances into our life, so it also attracts health – or not. Our body is also a mirror of our mind.

We have now been able to chart the movement of chemicals around the body that correspond to our mental and emotional states as well as the switching on and off of some of our genes. But the level at which the mind begins to affect the body goes much deeper than that.

Everything in your body is made of atoms, and the atoms themselves are made of tiny subatomic particles. And these are made of even smaller particles, which are made of even smaller ones. It's like the Russian dolls with a smaller one inside, and a smaller one inside that. How far does it go? Where does it all start?

I am drawn to the mystical view of this: it starts with consciousness. That is to say that at the most basic level consciousness is the substance that everything is made of. This is of course a million miles away from conventionally accepted scientific wisdom. And if it were really true, surely we'd all be able to just imagine something and it would materialize right in front of us. We'd be able to walk on water too, and turn water into wine, and…

I think we are heading in this direction and in time more people will view the world through spiritual eyes than through material eyes.

Throughout history there have been great masters who knew the deepest secrets of life and worked miracles. Only they weren't miracles to them – they were normal occurrences. Our ability to manipulate matter depends on how much we believe that we can. And we need to really, really believe. I'm not just talking of the way that you believe that you could run a mile in eight minutes. I'm talking about the level of certainty that knows that when you jump up you will come down again. I believe that we are moving in this direction. It might take a long time, but

I believe it's our destiny. Indeed, Christ said, 'You will do all that I have done and even greater things.'

Mind interacts with matter all the time. We just grow up without knowing it. Therefore we don't expect to be able to perform miracles. So most of us don't. But more and more people are stretching their abilities.

While I was organizing a charity event called Spirit Aid, during 2002, Uri Geller invited a few of us to his home. Not being able to resist the temptation, I took a spoon along and hoped it wouldn't be rude to ask Uri to demonstrate bending it. He rubbed it for a few seconds and it started to bend. Then he laid it on the ground and it continued to bend. It bent up like a boomerang in less than a minute. I was amazed. I still have it at home.

Nowadays there are workshops all around the world teaching people how to bend spoons and forks. Thousands of people can do it. Conventional science has no explanation for it, but it happens. It's a case of mind over matter, because at the most rudimentary level they are the same thing.

How to use the law of attraction

So how can all this help you? Say you have a dream. Start by getting really clear about it. You should be specific. Imagine it regularly. Chances are you'll daydream about it.

That's great. But just make sure that you don't think it's just a fantasy that can never happen. Every picture you create often enough in your mind will begin to form for real in your life. The seeds are planted right away and more often than not small things will begin to happen around you. Pay attention to these.

Some people prefer to set aside some time every day, or every other day, to formally imagine their dream. This is called visualization and it's a great exercise as it also shows that you are determined to make your dream happen.

I use what I call 'feelingization', where I *feel* how great it is to have what I want. A powerful emotional charge will always speed up the attraction process, just as strong emotions shift more chemicals in the body. We've already seen how more brain material is constructed by powerfully imagining something than by just thinking about it. So get excited and get enthusiastic about your dream. See it really happening.

If you find yourself complaining that you don't have it yet, stop! Complaining is one of the most efficient ways to hold back what you want. The law of attraction says that you attract what you think about, and if you're complaining, you're thinking about the fact that what you want is not here yet. So you get 'not here yet'. You attract not having it. You attract people and ideas that will guide you away from your goal.

It can take practice to catch yourself complaining and to find the strength to turn your thoughts around. Some people feel depressed about their whole life because their goals and dreams seem too far away.

If this is the case and you really can't find the strength you need, you might benefit from speaking to a doctor or therapist. Sometimes just talking helps. It's important to try to release your worry. If you feel like trying a book, I would recommend Byron Katie's *Loving What Is*. But why don't you try turning it around yourself first? What do you have to lose? You might have tried before and not got very far, but did you know about the law of attraction then? You do now. So there's a good chance that the outcome will be different.

Remember, too, that most people assume that they have to be positive to get what they want, and they beat themselves up when their mind strays. But being positive is really about having faith that you will get through any difficulties you may face, no matter what. That's real positivity.

And you know what? Often when you stop *trying* to change things and relax in the knowledge that you will get through it all eventually, whatever it is, maybe with the help of family or friends, or through faith in God or some other deity, or through faith in yourself, then things have a knack of changing by themselves. And this is because you have removed the emotional charge of not having your dream and have therefore allowed it to be attracted to you.

Sometimes, however, it is true that no matter how hard you try to attract your dream, things just don't change. There are times in life when you can't change a certain situation. So you are left with only one option – to change yourself. And maybe that was the whole point. Maybe that was part of your preincarnation plan. Maybe the situation that you can't change was something that you chose in order to gain a deeper spiritual understanding of life, or to develop more passion and determination, or courage, or faith, or compassion, or to become a completely new person – better, stronger, more confident, more beautiful, more generous and kind than you ever were before. Everything has a purpose.

But to help you to attract what you want in your life, in the next chapter I have distilled the law of attraction down to nine key principles.

Nine **Principles** for Inspired **Attraction**

I believe that we have unlimited potential to create what we want in life. But if you choose to focus your greater efforts on what inspires you, your life will head in the direction that optimizes your spiritual growth.

Therefore here are nine principles that can help you to attract the things that inspire you in life.

1. Attracting is much easier when you choose what inspires you

When you feel inspired it is usually because you are remembering something you planned during preincarnation. So it's on your internal map. This means there are two forces working for you: 1) the natural flow towards what's on your map and 2) your focus attracting it.

So look within yourself for what makes you feel good. Don't hold back. Dare to have a dream. The fact that you can imagine it and it makes you feel good means that it's possible for you. Maybe all you were waiting for was this reminder. Go for it!

2. The more you give, the more you receive

When you give, you make a statement that says 'I have', otherwise you wouldn't be able to give. When your attention, even unconsciously, is on 'I have' you attract more things to have.

So be generous in giving. Give what you can to help others in terms of physical things, but also give genuinely of yourself. Give your time, your patience, your undivided attention, your forgiveness, your compassion and your love. When you give those things you attract having them. Be grateful too for what's around you. A focus on gratitude attracts more reasons to be grateful. I can't think of a better focus. Be grateful for the people in your life and for the blessings that are all around you.

3. You are worthy of living your dreams

When I was younger I would look at people who were wealthy or in positions of authority and imagine that they were more deserving of the things they wanted than I was. I concluded this because it seemed to me that they got everything they wanted and that people did what they told them to do. I felt that I always had to settle for small things and that my opinion didn't count in the world. I couldn't imagine having what I thought was the success and happiness that they appeared to enjoy.

But I came to understand that no one is better than anyone else. We are all parts of God and all of us are born with a divine right to know happiness.

And if you look underneath your goals and dreams and get to the core of why you want them, you will find the force that inspires you – the reason why you want what you want. When you know the reason, happiness comes much more easily to you.

For instance, I wrote this book not so that it would get published or would sell a million copies (although that would be nice), but because I was inspired by a desire to understand and to teach.

4. Emotional charges speed things up and slow them down

Emotion can be thought of as e-motion, energy in motion. If, when you imagine what you want, you get enthusiastic and excited about what you see, you attach a positive emotional charge to it and this speeds things up, bringing it to you faster. I call attaching a positive emotional charge to my visualization 'feelingization'.

The brain grows in the same way. When you have a

powerful emotional experience, the brain physically encodes it according to the emotional intensity. The more intense the emotion, the more intensive the encoding.

5. Complaining slows things down

When you complain that something isn't here yet, not only are you focusing on not having it and attracting not having it, but you're putting an emotional charge on not having it, so you're doubly slowing it down and will get even more of 'not having it'.

So if you catch yourself complaining, try to focus your mind on something else for a while. Keep practising this – the more you do it, the better you will become at it. Wouldn't you like to be the Olympic champion of your own mind rather than letting pain dictate what happens to you?

6. A watched kettle never boils

If you check up every five minutes to see if your goal is there yet, you're eventually going to notice that it's not. And no matter how good you are at visualizing, your dominant thought is going to be 'It's not here yet', so that's what you'll attract. A watched kettle never boils, as the saying goes.

You don't need to be thinking about what you want all the time. It's important to get on with other things. Forget about it for a while.

It's OK to think about what you want periodically throughout the day, though. I daydream about my dreams a lot. I can't help it. The thoughts just pop into my head and they feel great. Just don't become obsessed. There's a big difference between pleasantly daydreaming about your goals and looking everywhere for examples of things going in the right direction. One attracts what you want and the other attracts what you don't want.

Just keep an eye on how you feel and you'll know if you're on the right track.

7. It's not personal

The law of attraction is like gravity. Gravity doesn't come down hard on people who've done bad things and less hard on people who devote themselves to charity. The law of attraction is equally impartial.

People often say things like 'That's not fair. He doesn't deserve that. I've been good to people but he's been double-crossing them.' But other people's behaviour is irrelevant. The law of attraction is impersonal. It works regardless of what you've been doing. You attract what you focus on. Everyone does. That's all!

8. Ups and downs are normal

Usually, when you start to visualize or feelingize, things move in the right direction for a while. But you sometimes get days, and even weeks, when all progress appears to have stopped. Sometimes things even seem to go backwards.

Don't be disheartened. Ups and downs are normal. Just push through it or wait out the storm, so to speak. Resist the temptation to think it's not working. You will probably find that things will start to work for you again soon and that it will be even better than before.

9. If you can't change something, change yourself

Sometimes we get the idea that having a certain thing would be great. Maybe someone else has it and you want it too, or you've read a book saying that you can have anything you want and so you picked something that you quite fancy. But maybe it doesn't fit with your internal map.

Who knows, you may be flowing along an important current which has certain key things and people just a little further on. If you try to attract something or someone that would pull you off the current, it sometimes doesn't work out because it's not the best thing for you. So sometimes there's a deeper reason why you don't have what you want yet. Remember the mantra 'Whatever happens is for the best.'

And there are times in life when, no matter how hard you try, you can't change the situation. You are then left with only one option – to change yourself. Most of the time that's the point of the situation you're in anyway.

So you can have the things you want in your life. I have also noticed that if I imagine others having good fortune then good fortune often comes to them in one way or another. This means that not only can you attract things you want for yourself, but you can attract things for other people too. Often you will attract important contacts that you are able to pass on to them or you will see situations in their life just change for the better.

Why not apply your ability to attract what you want to create an even better world for our children and our children's children? We have the ability to leave them a legacy to be proud of. We have the ability to attract peace in the world. We can also attract food and education for all. It starts with a dream!

It's Not your Fault

Sometimes people easily manage to make huge positive changes in their life. But others struggle. My good friend Liz Ivory made me laugh once when she said that she was a 'victim of personal development'. We learn all the tools and techniques, but we don't always find the ability to put them into practice in our own unique life situation. We carry on learning technique after technique, and the more new things we learn and aren't able to make work, the more inadequate we feel and the more we focus on what's wrong with us.

Sometimes circumstances, and our inability to change them, are not our fault. Sometimes hard times are on our map and we are unconsciously guided to them.

The very genetics that we are born with can influence the way we look at the world and respond to situations. Some people who have shown criminal behaviour, for instance, lack the genetic ability to produce enough serotonin in the brain to help them to resist urges and temptations.

Addictions can overpower a person's free will too. Some children are even born addicted to drugs because the mother has a drug habit. Very often people condemn addicts' behaviour without understanding that they have little control over it. Shaking off an addiction is not an easy thing to do. Have you ever had a really strong coffee? Did you speak quickly afterwards? Did you feel agitated? Did you feel spaced out? Were you able to just snap out of it? Have you ever drunk a lot of alcohol? Were you able to sober up in just a few minutes?

Remember too that some of our genetic tendencies are the product of the experiences of our great great grandparents. The way that we act in some situations is a result of the biochemical programming that we inherited from them.

In his book *The Biology of Transcendence*, Joseph Chilton Pearce showed photographs of brain scans of the prefrontal lobes of two people, one a non-violent person and the other a violent person. The prefrontal lobes are the part of the brain that evolved most recently. They control the higher brain functions. In the non-violent person they were dense with neurons, but in the violent person the density of neurons was markedly different. That person's prefrontal lobes were much less developed, indicating that they had much less control over their behaviour.

So, in effect, some people who exhibit violent behaviour do so because their genes do not promote the full growth of the prefrontals. Prefrontal lobes also tend to be less dense if children are brought up in an angry and violent environment. Is this their fault? And what are we to do with people who use violence? Rather than being dismissive or judgemental, we need to look at how we can help. Rehabilitation, training and compassion would go a lot further towards creating a peaceful society than locking people up and throwing away the key. As a society, we could take a more evolved and understanding approach.

Depression, too, needs understanding. When I was a child my mum had post-natal depression after the birth of my sister Lynn, the youngest of my three sisters, and it lasted for many years. It was made worse because in the 1970s it wasn't well recognized where we lived. The typical response my mum got from friends, doctors and psychiatrists was 'Give yourself a shake' or 'Pull yourself together.' It was well meant, but expecting someone with depression to shake themselves out of it is like expecting a person with a broken leg to go out for a jog and 'just run it off'. I experienced a six-month bout of depression myself in 1998 and remember coming home from work every day, pulling the curtains shut, lying on the floor and having a cry. It is a miracle to me that my mother got through the years of post-natal depression. It is testimony to her great inner strength.

Some studies into post-natal depression have shown that it can result from a deficiency of EPA in the brain. EPA is an omega-3 fatty acid that you can get from oily fish. A foetus needs it for the growth of its brain and if the mother's diet is not rich in it then the foetus will get what it needs from the mother's brain. So after the birth the mother's brain can lack EPA and depression can result. David Servan-Schreiber, who is Clinical Professor of Psychiatry at the University of Pittsburgh School of Medicine, explains this very well in his excellent book *Healing without Freud or Prozac*.

If my mum had been in a different emotional space after the birth of my sister she would probably have been more confident and able to do some things differently. Perhaps she would have been able to attract financial abundance, but in her emotional state that was next to impossible. But the circumstances that she did attract during this time were not her fault. The power was there. It always is. It's just that, at times, we lack the strength or the know-how to use it. We shouldn't be blamed for this. It's not our fault.

It was meant to be

Our internal map guides us to people, places and circumstances that we chose before birth to serve as a playground for our growth. But we didn't choose them consciously. After birth we are no longer aware of our choices, so cannot be held accountable for them.

There may have been many reasons for our choices. Some souls may have chosen difficult conditions to teach humanity compassion, while others may have chosen, say, poverty or illness because in previous lifetimes they experienced abundance and health. Some events are part of our maps and from our current perspective we aren't able to understand the deeper reasons behind them. Sometimes we need to just look at things, say, 'It happened – it was meant to be' and get on with our life.

If you have been through a difficult experience, the important thing to focus on now is what you gained from it. It may have prepared you for the next chapter of your life. Perhaps this preparation was the whole point. And how you choose to respond from now on will determine the tone of events that you attract from now on.

If you are trying to attract new things and finding it difficult to make changes, even in yourself, don't let it get you down. Sometimes you just need to ride out the wave, so to speak. You might use the thought 'This too will pass' to give yourself some comfort or tell yourself, 'No matter what, I can get through this.' I have repeated this many, many times in my own life.

Nothing lasts forever. Change is inevitable. Eventually, no matter how long it takes, things will change. Ultimately, even the physical body will cease and the spirit will fly again.

Your power

In the meantime, sometimes life can seem out of control. You take one personal setback after another, smacking into rocks on your journey down the river. And you didn't consciously create any of the collisions. You didn't consciously choose the rocks. How unfair is that?!

Many events happen to us for one of two reasons:

1. They are on our internal map.
2. Our personal mental and emotional climate creates a flow that leads us into certain circumstances.

If events are on our internal map, there is a high probability that they will happen. But the forces of destiny and the power of free will work together. Remember that we have the free will to change our maps.

We also have control over our mental and emotional climate. So, if you are experiencing setbacks, try changing what you focus on. You may have tuned yourself in to a negative mental and emotional current. Even if it is a strong current, you needn't let it sweep you away. If you change your mind, you can create a new current through the law of attraction.

And when you decide to attract something better for yourself, it amplifies your ability to swim with the tide. It's as if you have turned into an Olympic swimmer overnight!

Leaving the past behind

Sometimes we are tuned into a mental and emotional climate of fear because of our past experiences, so we attract more reasons to be fearful.

Whenever an issue is unresolved in us we tend to attract more of the same until we do resolve it. That's because we are focused on the pain of it. If you still feel pain or anger over an abusive episode from your past then you increase the probability that you will attract a similar situation in the future. You might attract another abusive partner, for instance, or find yourself in a job where you are bullied. But when you resolve the issue, you attract completely different people and circumstances.

Often people blame themselves for being abused. This was highlighted in one of my favourite films, *Good Will Hunting*, featuring Matt Damon, Ben Affleck and Robin Williams. When Robin Williams's character finally got Will (Matt Damon) to realize that being beaten by his father was not his fault, he was able to move forward in his life. He was able to leave that current of the river. And you can get help and move on, just as Will did.

Many people, though, are caught in a mental and emotional dilemma. They don't want to accept that the law of attraction is real because then they conclude that all the bad things that have occurred in their life were their fault. So they convince themselves that everything that happens is meant to be or is God's will and that they have no control over events. It's less painful that way. However, by passing everything over to fate they render themselves powerless because they affirm that they have no control over their lives – and so they don't.

But if a person hasn't been aware of how thoughts attract then they can't be held accountable for the bad things they have attracted in the past. That would be like holding a two-year-old child accountable for a knocking over a table when it is barely able to walk and talk.

You don't need to hold yourself accountable for what's happened in the past. You don't even need to hold others accountable. You just need to recognize how amazing and powerful you are now and to use the law of attraction to create what you want in your life from this moment onwards. Maybe recognizing this, now, was part of your plan. Maybe it was on your internal map. Maybe you were meant to read this book at this exact moment.

When you do gain control of your thoughts then you need to accept much more responsibility, of course. That's the hard bit. It is a daring act to move into responsibility, because you need to examine the events that happen to you in the context of what you were thinking about or focusing on in the time leading up to them.

Many people prefer not to know how powerful their thoughts are for fear of having to accept responsibility. But I invite you, now, to take your head out of the sand. Only when you gain control over your own mind, and life, are you able to help everyone else create a better world.

Mass Destiny

We may all have the ability to shape our individual lives, but what of our common future? We share the same planet, so the destiny of humanity is shared by all of us.

In his book *Same Soul, Many Bodies*, psychiatrist Brian Weiss described common futures that his patients described while undergoing hypnotic progression. Weiss progressed thousands of patients, who described life 100 or 200 years from now, 300–600 years from now and about 1,000 years from now. The reason the years aren't exact is that it's difficult to put an exact time on the future because it is so fluid. It changes with every act we take now, which is a good thing. It's not set in stone. Therefore these futures may never happen. Nevertheless there was a high degree of similarity in what the patients saw.

In around 100–200 years from now, according to Weiss's patients, life is similar to how it is now. There is less disease and more pollution, and global warming is still an issue. There have also been a number of natural and man-made disasters between now and then. Presumably these have been the result of global warming.

The picture deteriorates somewhere between 300 and 600 years into the future and humanity enters a dark age. The progressions of some people indicated that this time period could be much closer, however, maybe even soon. During it the human population is substantially lower, which Dr Weiss proposes could be due to a decline in fertility rates, possibly caused by chemical toxins in our food, air and water.

Around 1,000 years from now – although, once again, this could be closer or farther away due to the fluidity of time – the future is much brighter. We live in a beautiful, peaceful, fertile and much greener world. The population is still lower than it is now, but maybe that's because we've seen no need to increase it. We live in an evolved state of consciousness and there is no violence, war or poverty.

Could this happen, and perhaps even sooner than Dr Weiss's patients saw? Earlier on, I mentioned the Mayan civilization. Their calendar ends on 21 December 2012, a date that is known as the end of time. It is the end of an age of 5,200 years that began in 3114 BC. According to Lonnie Thomson, a professor of geological sciences at

Ohio State University, the Earth underwent an abrupt climate catastrophe around 5,200 years ago. It is interesting that we are facing a potential climate catastrophe again now. And this is something that affects us all. It is a collective destiny.

I believe that, astrologically, 21 December 2012 is significant. It has meaning in the collective unconscious. It is the beginning of a new age or a new cycle. But what we do in this new cycle is up to us. If we want a world to be proud of then we have to create it. We do have that power. We don't need to experience the futures that Dr Weiss's patients saw.

Changing the mental and emotional climate

I like to think of a person's average mental and emotional state as their mental and emotional climate. Have you ever seen those cartoons where an unhappy character is followed around by a rain cloud? That character has an unhappy mental and emotional climate.

Each person's thoughts ripple outwards, like a pebble dropped in a pond, mixing and merging with the waves created by everyone else's. They set up vibrations across the spider's web. However you like to think of it, we are all connected. So I believe that we share a collective mental and emotional climate that represents the average mental and emotional state of humanity. Just as rain clouds mix, so do our mental and emotional clouds.

On an individual level, the state of a person's climate prompts the law of attraction to bring them events and people that mirror that climate. If their climate is unhappy then they tend to attract more events and people that keep them unhappy. Similarly, if their climate is positive then they tend to attract events and people that help them to be even more positive. A positive intention, even when your climate is sad, however, can attract a glimmer of hope. It will immediately set the wheels in motion for you to have it. But in general, events mirror our mental and emotional climates.

Just as this happens on an individual scale, so it happens on a mass scale – we attract collective events that mirror our collective mental and emotional climate. So conflicts and wars in our hearts and minds will create the climate that allows mass conflicts and wars to take place in the world. Every thought of hatred sends a vibration through the web that joins with other thoughts of hatred and a 'hatred cloud' begins to form that colours the collective mental and emotional climate. When it gains enough strength, it reaches a tipping point and a conflict or war breaks out. Similarly, love in our hearts and minds will create a climate that promotes co-operation, tolerance and kindness.

Local climates, like a home, office, village, town or nation, create local events first before they start to filter out to more of the world. A lot of conflict in your personal climate can sometimes lead to conflict in your office environment, for instance. And it's not just your climate – it's other people's too. Together you germinate the mental and emotional seeds that grow into an unhappy place to work in.

If you change your own climate, though, you can just as easily tip the local climate to one of fun, happiness and productivity. If you have the discipline to correct your thinking, your attitude and your behaviour, you will influence the climate of people around you. This is why a person of evolved consciousness can shift the atmosphere of most places they enter just by their presence. People nearby just start to feel different.

Looking at the global situation today, it is a sobering thought that we collectively created the war against terrorism experience. That is an outer reflection of our own personal lack of tolerance towards other people's beliefs. And not just religious beliefs, but also beliefs about what we think the right lifestyle should be, what the right kind of diet should be, which political party is the right one, which political system is the right one, which healing system is the right one and which scientific belief system is the right one. It's all too common for people to angrily dismiss other people's beliefs as inadequate. But any dismissal of another person's right to believe what they want is disrespectful and fuels other kinds of division in the world because it sends out vibrations that inspire other people to be dismissive of others' views. It's OK to disagree over what works best, but not to the extent that you show a lack of respect.

Perhaps we were all born into currents that we could see would take us to where we are now. The challenge we chose was to learn to live together and work together, side by side, regardless of race or belief system – to recognize that we are all part of the same human family and understand that everyone deserves respect. Maybe that was the point of the terrorism experience that we now face.

So if we want to change the world for the better it really does start with us as individuals. It takes discipline to break a 'habit of a lifetime', but just remember that you attract what you focus on. If you don't like what you're attracting then you must change what you hold in your heart and mind.

When you do change, your new focus sends vibrations throughout the web and new clouds begin to form in the collective mental and emotional climate. These mix with other people's clouds and inspire them to change things about themselves too. Never underestimate your own power. Resist the temptation to see yourself as small in any way, no matter what society might tell you.

Mass currents

Just as we are born with an individual map that guides the flow of our own individual current in the ocean, so our current is part of a mass, or collective, current that flows in the direction that we have collectively chosen and are collectively choosing now.

Each of us is born into our own current that sits within the mass current. The mass current is hardly noticeable, however. It doesn't restrict our freedom. We still have the free will to choose what we want. But it does affect individual currents in such a way that we experience what it flows towards.

Think about it in this way. The Earth is moving in a circle around the sun. We experience what this movement brings. It doesn't affect how we go about our daily business. But if the Earth were to pass through a field of asteroids, that might affect us. We might get big rocks landing on our cars.

So if the collective current takes us to a war, it affects all of us, though some people's individual currents will get caught up in the collective current more than others. The ones at the centre will be affected the most, while those at the edges will hardly be touched.

Also, just as our individual unconscious minds form a collective unconscious mind, so our individual souls are part of a collective soul. It is the soul of humanity. And just as your bigger soul, or oversoul, experiences every possible current your life could flow along, so the oversoul of humanity experiences every possible direction of the mass current.

Before we are born, we can see where the collective current is flowing. If it's flowing towards peace, love, sharing and enlightenment, developing the necessary knowledge and skills for finding these qualities in our own hearts will be part of our individual maps, so we will be led to people, books and realizations that will help this development. We will also be guided towards making the right decisions. If the wrong people happen to be in power then they will lose that power as people who can make an enlightened difference take their places.

If the collective current is flowing towards disaster, however, our internal maps will be guiding us towards making the errors of judgement that ensure that happens. Our spiritual goals will then concern how we deal with the situation, how we get through it and who we can become in the midst of the great challenges it presents to us.

But whatever the current when we were born, it might have changed direction several times since. If you were born at a time when the current was taking us all into a dark age and it has now changed to look much more promising then you will be inspired with new knowledge and new skills that will allow you to play a role in shaping the new destiny for humanity. You will set a new direction for your personal current and will receive all the inspiration you need from your guides.

There are many stories of children being born now who are more spiritually advanced than at any previous time. Some have been affectionately called indigo children. Many tend to be intelligent yet disruptive. Some are rebelling against any kind of authority, because they intuitively understand that they should be treated more respectfully. Instead of being told what to do, they want to be asked. Then they'll do it, because you asked. It is just about respect.

As they become teenagers, it bothers them that the world's systems seem to be geared more towards profit than the welfare of people or the environment. They rebel against leaders who make decisions that serve personal or national interest at the expense of the whole. They retain more of an intuitive memory of the other side than most adults do and therefore have more of a understanding that we are all part of the same family. They intuitively understand that the best way forward is for everyone to have equal opportunities and be treated with equal respect, regardless of race, religion, background or status.

Other such 'advanced' children are not so rebellious. They have a natural air of peace or wisdom about them. When people look into their eyes they often comment that they are 'old souls'.

The birth of such children may be a sign that the mass current is taking us to a better place than the one we're currently in. Their thoughts and intentions will help to tilt the collective mental and emotional climate towards peace, happiness, sharing and joy, and will help all of us to attract more positive events. But we still need to help, otherwise we could tilt the current another way. We need to bring more peace and love into our own hearts and minds and let them colour our actions.

It's up to us

Of all the futures that exist for us, the one that we experience is the one that we collectively choose. It will be the one that reflects what we hold in our hearts and minds. It will reflect our thoughts, emotions, desires, ideas, beliefs and actions.

Many people believe that our world is heading into darkness on account of our behaviour. Looking at how international economic systems seem to benefit the rich and make the poor poorer, how large corporations plunder the planet and pollute the environment and how we personally consume resources at an alarming rate and endanger our climate through our overuse of fossil fuels, it's easy to be pessimistic. But we could still turn it around. We could create a new mass current.

Maybe the mass current is heading towards enlightened times. Maybe there's darkness to go through first. I don't personally know what lies ahead of us. The future is fluid. Maybe the visions of Dr Weiss's patients are accurate for where we are heading right now. Maybe the people who believe the end of the current age of the Mayan calendar means there will be disaster are right. Or maybe there will be a shift in consciousness instead and it will be the start of a period of spiritual enlightenment.

I think the future changes a lot. I think we are on a knife-edge at the moment and it could tip either way. It could be disaster or it could be joy. But I do know that if we choose to bring more love into our own hearts and minds then there is only one future that we can know. But it's up to us all! What do you choose?

10 What's the Point?

Individual destiny and mass destiny may flow one way or another, but what is it all for? What's the purpose? What's the point?

Everything happens for a reason

To recap, as we go through life, for most of us it's about getting from A to B. But while it's great to get to B, it is the bit in between that's important. This is where the real work is done. This is the message from people who have had NDEs and from people who have undergone hypnotic regression and progression.

We set ourselves goals and challenges before we are born that are intended to serve as the scaffolding for our spiritual evolution. They are not set in stone. Our map inspires us to create the necessary events, but we don't have to if we choose not to. But regardless of what we choose, our life is always the perfect playground for our evolution.

Say I decided that I wanted to work on forgiveness, for instance, to deepen my knowledge and experience of it. I've used this as an example because it's something that I've had to do.

Once I often attracted bullying situations. And in these situations, I was not alone. The bully, or bullies, had to play a role too. Often bullies are people who forget themselves and go down a violent or bullying path that was not on their map. If you have chosen to experience bullying, you will sense who these people are and will be unconsciously attracted to them. But sometimes people are born with bullying on their map. It takes great soul friendship for this. Think of it this way. Could you imagine asking one of your friends to punch you on the nose so that you could learn to rise above pain? It would take real friendship for this. Sometimes this is what we do before birth – we make agreements that we will hurt each other in order to learn. And maybe we'll swap roles in the next life so that we can see things from the other perspective.

After the plan has been agreed, when we are born our internal maps will draw us together. If we have a bullying plan, we might end up working together or being at the same school. My 'friend', for reasons unknown to himself at a conscious level, just won't like me, or will be jealous of me, and won't be able to resist making my life very difficult. He will bully me repeatedly. At first this will be painful for me, but eventually – and this might take days, weeks, months or even years – I will be able to see him through different eyes and forgive him. That is the whole point.

Can you imagine the look on a bully's face if you were to say calmly, 'Thank you for giving me the opportunity to know forgiveness'? It might just stir a memory in them that would help them to leave bullying behind. It might be the cue they were unconsciously waiting for. It might be your part of the deal!

Why bad things happen to good people

Some events are extremely painful, but they do have a purpose. A child might be born to loving parents but only live a short time, for example. Although this would be extremely hard to deal with at the time, the parents might later come to believe that the soul of the child entered their life for a reason. It might have touched them in some way that changed them forever. That might have been what that soul intended. That was its gift to them.

To take another example, some people are born into extreme poverty where every day is a struggle for survival.

Nevertheless they may have chosen those extreme circumstances for their own evolutionary reasons. In those circumstances they may have roles that serve their own needs and that of the immediate community. Some might be providers, protectors, mothers, teachers or leaders – all co-operating in a way that ensures the survival and growth of their community and the fulfilment of each other's spiritual goals.

People born into such extreme circumstances are still able to use the law of attraction, but it is usually applied to immediate needs like food, shelter and survival rather than jobs, homes, new careers and cars.

A secondary purpose of people born into these sorts of conditions might be to help other people to discover their compassion and generosity. On seeing their poverty, many millions of people might be inspired to take some kind of action to make things better for their fellow humans. Many of the souls on the televised news reports of poverty in Africa, for instance, would have chosen to be there to highlight what humanity had allowed to happen and to help most others to reach inside themselves and find a deeper level of compassion than ever before. When I say they chose it, I most definitely do not mean that they had any conscious memory of it – it was all done before birth. But they chose it all the same. In my opinion it takes a loving, advanced and courageous soul to make such a choice. It may be a huge gift to humanity.

Knowing the point of life from another soul's perspective is no excuse for brushing another's plight away, however. They may have chosen that life, but in their immediate experience they are feeling pain. Imagine that you had had a bad fall but people just walked past and ignored you lying there because they imagined that you had chosen to do that for your own spiritual evolution. Maybe you actually had, but that wouldn't alter the fact that you were in pain and would appreciate someone coming along and helping you!

To take another example, many people go through painful marriage break-ups. At the time there can be depression and anger, especially if one person has left the other. But be assured that your ex-partner came into your life for a reason. Maybe the relationship was only ever meant to last for a short time, to help you work on some aspect of your spiritual development, or to prepare you for the next person in your life, or even to give you some children. Some people are only meant to be with us for a while and that is the plan, even if it's hard to take at the time. Once their work is done, they go out of our life as quickly as they came into it.

At the time it's easy to say that one or the other of you caused the break-up. But say it was on both your map and your ex-partner's. Therefore neither of you was at fault. It was meant to happen. You would have been unconsciously drawn to a partner who would be likely to leave you at a later date and your partner would have been unconsciously drawn to someone that they would leave. And neither of you would have been consciously aware of what was to come, otherwise you wouldn't have had the meaningful relationship that you did. We resort to blame for many things in life. But every time we do we further distance ourselves from our soul.

I'm not advocating letting everyone off. Holding someone accountable for their actions is important for *their* journey of learning about honesty, integrity and trust. But if their actions involved you then there's a good chance that the situation was on your map and you felt that it would help you on *your* journey.

From this perspective you can focus on the lessons that you learned about yourself. You can forgive and move on. Maybe one day you'll even thank your ex-partner for helping you on your journey.

Out of time

Imagine a drop of paint was falling onto a canvas, but on the way down it hits the tip of a brush and breaks into two drops. They both land on the canvas at the same time, a few inches apart. Now for this metaphor the canvas represents your life journey from birth to death and the two drops represent you and a goal.

As time passes, you travel across the canvas to reach your goal. When you get there, you see the other drop for the first time. To you, it didn't exist until you arrived at that spot and 'created' it. But looking down from above, 'out of time', both of you landed on the canvas at the same 'time'. Remember, time doesn't exist for your soul.

Because you wanted to achieve that goal, the law of attraction drew you together through time and space. From your perspective, thoughts formed in your mind about the goal and then you attracted it. From another perspective, the goal attracted you, just as you could say that a marriage break-up caused an affair that led to it. It's like a whirlpool up ahead on a river. It gently pulls you forward.

From out of time, from your soul's perspective, neither is true. Each causes the other. Each is necessary for the existence of the other.

The point of understanding life like this is to step out of time. That's where your soul is. And that's where you're heading. We all are.

Stepping out of time also moves you into a space of trust. It gets rid of the undercurrent of fear that most people live with and the feeling of separation. When you are out of time, you know that you are connected to everyone and everything. You're all part of the same ocean.

Normally we spend our lives seeking to create, create and create, and mostly from a feeling of lack – 'I'm not there yet' or 'I don't have enough' or 'I need such and such a thing to be fulfilled.' The law of attraction is a wonderful tool that helps us to attract our dreams and to realize the power we have to create our own life. But in and of itself it does not bring fulfilment.

When you are out of time, though, there is no one and nothing that is not part of you. So you are connected to all the things that you dream of. At this level you know that if you imagine something, it will come to you, and if it doesn't then something even better will. Your inner wisdom will always guide you to what is ultimately best for your spiritual development.

From out of time the point isn't what you do, it's who you are as you do it. It's who or what you are being right now that counts. Being out of time focuses you on the present moment. You stop ruminating about the past or worrying about the future.

A lot of people feel caught in the dilemma that they can either attract what they want or follow a spiritual path. When attracting, they put spiritual thoughts aside, and when immersed on the spiritual path, they reject all past hopes and dreams. But when you step out of time and align with your soul, you are inspired with spiritual thoughts and actions – forgiveness, compassion, generosity, kindness and love. And more often than not you also follow your dreams.

You still create your reality with the law of attraction. It's impossible not to. But you realize that everything that's happening right now is perfect, both for your growth and for the growth of everyone else. This means that what you perceive to be good things and bad things are all perfectly pitched at the right level for people to learn forgiveness, compassion, and so on. It's all happening to take all of us to the next level of our spiritual evolution.

God's will vs your will

Your soul evolves through your experiences. And as it is evolving, it is reaching inside itself. Just as you go inside yourself and come to know yourself as your soul, so your soul comes to know itself as everything – All That Is. In many cultures, this is God. Your soul evolves to become God.

And God evolves too. Just as your soul evolves through service to you, so God evolves through service to your soul, and to you. Think of it as God serving His children (your soul and other souls) and grandchildren (you and me). At the beginning of time God sent out fragments of Himself that would take an epic journey through time and space back to God again. The initial fragments, being part of God, had an inbuilt attractive force that would lead them home again. They wanted to unite with the whole again. This was the root of the law of attraction – a deep unconscious remembering that once they existed as one with everything and one day they would be one with the whole again.

And so every path leads back to the whole. It is impossible not to get there because the memory of who we are draws us there. It doesn't matter whether you take the high road or the low road, whether you go over land, air or sea, or whether you are Catholic, Hindu, Muslim or any other religion, you will get there eventually. It is the quality of your experiences that accelerates you on your journey, not the number of miles that you cover, the vehicle that you drive to get there or the houses that you stay in along the way. God doesn't require you to take one path over another. It's all up to you. Some paths might be easier than others, but none is a requirement. You can't fail to get home again. That is the only thing in the infinite field of possibilities that's not possible.

And so God doesn't have a will, or a preference, for you. You are part of the whole, so ultimately your will is God's will. The spirit of God has substance, however. It is the substance of love in the highest, grandest, most intense and spectacular sense. It can only be described as infinite love. When you surrender to the spirit of God, you align yourself completely with love. It then feels as though you are doing God's will, and in a sense you are, but it's actually your will. Because you are so infused with this spirit, you are merely choosing higher things.

When you are aligned with love, the thoughts that form in your mind are coloured with love. You notice that people around you are part of God too. You see God everywhere around you and because that is what you focus on, you create love, beauty and perfection everywhere you go. This is the path taken by all great spiritual masters.

So surrendering to God doesn't mean giving up your free will. Instead, you are inspired to use your free will to create go(o)d things.

The comfort factor

It is easy when you approach this whole subject in an analytical way, which many people do, to remove the personal touch from God. We see God as a force or a field, the universe or an infinite field of consciousness, but we forget that being infinitely conscious means being infinitely loving and intelligent.

Think of a time when you were at your most loving, or kindest, or most forgiving, or most compassionate. Now multiply that by a million. That isn't even close to the level of love, kindness, forgiveness or compassion that God feels. Think of when you were at your most intelligent. Now multiply this by a million. Again, you can't even begin to approach the level of intelligence of God.

For the purposes of writing this book I could easily have stuck to terms like 'infinite field of consciousness' or 'universe', so that non-religious people would not be offended. I am not religious myself, though I would say that I am spiritual. I have chosen to talk about God because personally I need to know that there is an infinite intelligence, like a parent, looking after us, loving us and serving us; and to which we can talk at any time – not just a force or a field, but a person. Although God is much more than a person, seeing God as a person reminds me of God's humanity. Sometimes it's so comforting just to know that there's someone, or something, out there with your best interests at heart.

I'm not suggesting that you suddenly start going to church or become a religious or spiritual zealot. I am only suggesting that you find a way of considering that the infinite field of consciousness is alive and that you show tolerance towards other people's preferred way of understanding it. You might still use your preferred terms, but just add the life to it in your mind. I personally prefer to call it God and hope that no one is offended by my preferred way of understanding life.

And one of the most comforting things about God is that He will answer your prayers.

How to pray

A friend of mine once sent me one of those circular e-mails that fly around the world several times. I couldn't find its source, but I am grateful to whomever started it because I found it inspirational. It said that God only ever answered prayers in one of three ways:

1. Yes.
2. Not yet.
3. I have something better in mind.

When you ask something of God, you invite the spirit of love in the highest possible sense, so you receive what is ultimately best for you and for everyone concerned. This is why it sometimes feels as though you don't always get what you want.

Another reason for this is that many people pray to God to make something happen. But asking God to make something happen is a negative presupposition. It presupposes that you have no power to make it happen yourself. And you have.

The law of attraction, as we have seen, follows your thoughts. So, like a negative placebo effect (the nocebo effect), your belief in your powerlessness attracts a feeling of powerlessness, people who make you feel weak and situations in which you appear to have little or no control. When you pray with a belief that you are powerless you often find that you can't get out of situations you appear to be stuck in. You simply wait in the hope that God will say 'yes' this time.

A much more powerful prayer is to ask God to *help you* to create what you want. That way you still ask for help, but you also positively affirm that you are the instrument and that you have the power to make it happen. You're just asking for a wee helping hand. Ask God to help you to see it. If you can see it in your mind then it's already on its way.

The simplest way to think of it is instead of praying *for* something, just *pray* it. Praying *for* something affirms that it isn't here yet, otherwise why would you be praying for it? And so, by the law of attraction, you create not having it, or at least you slow down its arrival. The momentum of your desire is weakened by the affirmation that it's not here yet.

To *pray* something, just see and feel that it is happening. Visualizing something happening and something actually happening both light up the same neurons in the brain. The brain can't tell the difference. Neither can the law of attraction. It just attracts what you see. That is the secret of prayer that has been passed down via word of mouth in many great spiritual traditions.

When you pray something, you can still talk to God. You can say thank you for helping you to 'see' what you want, you can ask for help in attracting it and you can just have a general chat. You can pour your heart out if you want to. That's good too. And when you've finished, ask for help and pray it, and you will be helped in whatever way is best for you.

11
Count your Blessings

I travelled to India a few years ago and visited a few small villages at the foot of some mountains in Rajasthan. A year earlier I travelled to Peru and visited some small villages there too. One thing that stuck in my mind from both trips was seeing children laughing and playing. They seemed genuinely happy. Yet, to us, they lived in poverty. They didn't have the same toys that most kids I knew back home had. They didn't have PlayStations or Xboxes or computers.

When I was growing up in the seventies, we didn't have these either. Toys were much simpler and we spent our time outside, playing games like tag, dodge ball and football. The girls played, too, and they also played games like hopscotch and Chinese ropes, where they strung coloured elastic bands together and jumped over them, getting progressively higher and higher.

Seeing the children in India and Peru reminded me that happiness has nothing to do with what you have. No matter what you have, it is what you do with it that makes you feel good. I remember a few Christmases ago watching one of my nephews getting more pleasure out of the Christmas wrapping paper than the toy inside it. The paper made a great sound and he could crumple it with his hands and throw it. It was even more fun for him when I joined in the game of 'wrapping paper', which we played for the next half-hour, leaving all the more expensive presents on the table untouched.

It's what you focus on that makes you feel good. If a child has a colouring book it might take great pleasure in it. I certainly did when I was young. But if that child had hoped for a bicycle then it might not enjoy playing with the colouring book. And if it had a bicycle but hoped for a computer then it might not enjoy the bicycle as much.

As adults, we do the same thing. If we don't have the stuff we want, we focus on not having it and that makes us feel bad. Yet prior to the thought of not having it we might have been quite happy with what we had. Can't we just switch our minds back and pretend that we didn't want it in the first place?

My mum gave me a great teaching when I was little. We weren't financially well-off. We were a working-class family living in a council house on a council estate in a little village called Banknock in central Scotland. Whenever my three sisters or I complained about not having something, my mum would say, 'You should be thankful for what you've got,' and she would remind us of children in Africa who had much less. As a consequence I grew up with little desire to have all the 'stuff' that most people crave. We did get 'stuff' when we were young, the same as everyone else on our estate, but I learned to appreciate it. And looking back, how my mum and dad managed was a miracle. I have stuff now, but I don't crave the accumulation of it. I don't 'need' the latest gadgets and technology. I use them. They come in handy. But I can look at them and honestly say, 'It's great having you, but I don't need you to be happy.'

Being thankful for what we have is a very healthy attitude. Gratitude does wonders for the mind, body and soul. When you are grateful for who is in your life and what is in your life then by the law of attraction you attract more reasons to be grateful.

It also aids your nervous system and improves your immune system. In my first book, *It's The Thought That Counts*, I gave some of the scientific evidence for the healing power of love and gratitude on the body. Have you ever taken a big breath and paid attention to the great feeling of the air entering your lungs?

For many people, realizing what they have comes too late. It's only when someone or something is no longer in their life that they realize what they had. And it's all too easy to take people for granted. We sometimes miss out on quality times with our loved ones because even though we're with them physically, we're not really there. Our minds are elsewhere, mulling over the day's problems or feeling angry about not being respected. Weeks, months and years can go by and we've been with our loved ones in body but not in soul. So we miss out on the joy that comes from spending quality time with them.

One of my favourite films is *Liar, Liar*, starring Jim Carrey. His character is focused so much on his career that he is always cancelling seeing his son. He even misses his birthday party because he is climbing up the career ladder by having sex with his boss. The turning point comes when he feels that he is a bad father. He changes his priorities and begins to put his son first. As a consequence his life becomes richer and he gets back with his ex-wife, whom he has never stopped loving.

Life gets so much better when we notice what's right here in front of us. Little miracles occur.

Martin Luther King once said:

> *'If a man is called to be a street sweeper, he should sweep streets even as Michelangelo painted, or Beethoven composed music, or Shakespeare wrote poetry. He should sweep streets so well that all the hosts of heaven and earth will pause to say, "Here lived a great street sweeper who did his job well."'*

How many people do you know who take pride in what they do? Not that many, I reckon. You can tell the ones who do. They have a smile upon their faces and people want to be around them. They have an 'air' or a 'quality' about them that makes people feel good in their presence. The difficulty most people have with taking pride in what they do is that they want something else. The grass is always greener on the other side. If a person is in a job but has their heart set on a different job, their performance in their current job usually begins to drop. They are not happy in their job because they want another one. But the focus on not having what they want just attracts even more reasons to be unhappy.

Sometimes what unconsciously drives people in these situations is that they want to reach a breaking-point of unhappiness so they'll have the excuse, motivation, energy and conviction to do something about it. So they unconsciously keep on hating what they do now. OK, this works sometimes, but the downside is that you miss out on some of your life while you mull over all the reasons why you are unhappy. You don't have to hate the present to change it. There is another way. If you put your heart and soul into what you do now then things will begin to change in your life. And this is because you are beginning to change. And if things still don't change and you are still unhappy then take a positive action to change it.

So be grateful for what you have. Gratitude will bring you

even more reasons to be grateful. Who knows what they'll be? But once we've released the fear and negativity that we've built up around our hopes and dreams not having happened yet, they are free to come our way. Maybe your renewed pride in your work will be noticed by more senior members of the company and you will be offered bigger projects, or you'll be made redundant so you can pursue the dream you've always had. If you put everything into your family life, your relationships and your friendships, maybe a new relationship or other blessing will come your way. Miracles will happen. But they are not randomly bestowed by an external force. They happen *because of you*. They happen because of the change in you.

12 Be the Miracle

All around us the world is changing every day. How can we make the changes that we want? How can we have a world full of love, generosity, forgiveness, compassion and acceptance? Does that sound like a miracle to you? If you want to have a world like this then you need to *be* the miracle.

It's the small things that change the world because they happen around us every day. Most of the time we barely notice them. Make a point of noticing the love, generosity, forgiveness, compassion and acceptance you see every day and let the memory of them inspire you.

On the news and in the papers we often see retribution and fighting back on a grand scale. But you don't need to follow that example. You can set a different example for others to follow. It takes a bigger person to be an example of peace.

What isn't often shown on the news is that there are people everywhere resisting the temptation of a knee-jerk revenge reaction when someone has hurt or offended them. They know that only by setting an example of peace can they hope to heal the hurts on both sides. So they turn the other cheek. These people are all around you.

If someone has hurt or offended you at home, at work or in your social circle, what do you choose to do? Someone has to make the first move towards peace. Someone has to have the courage. Let it be you. Be the miracle.

Change starts with each of us, in our hearts and minds, before it becomes the dominant power in the world. If we bring love into our hearts, we can bring it into the world. Instead of nations being superpowers, let love and peace be the superpowers. They always have been. It's just that we have forgotten it. Let's remember just how powerful they are.

You can be active in demonstrating peace and love. When you are kind to someone, you never know how far that act travels and how many people are touched by it. A kind thing will change how they feel. Maybe they've had a bad day and your words or actions will lift them up. Without your kindness they might have gone on to take out their pain on their loved ones, who might then have continued the cycle. Your words or actions might have changed all that. You never know.

Have you ever had a hard day and then had someone say or do something really nice for you? It might seem small, but it touches you. It changes your day.

Pay it forward

I love the concept of 'paying it forward', which is where you do something kind for someone and when they want to show their gratitude by doing something in return for you, you suggest that they pay it forward instead by doing something kind for someone else. And when that person wants to show gratitude, it is paid forward too.

Last year my partner Elizabeth and I took a holiday in Italy and we flew first from Edinburgh to Dublin before catching a flight to Bologna. When we were in the departure lounge waiting to board our Bologna flight, I was feeling really thirsty. I noticed a vending machine that dispensed bottles of water so I went to get myself a bottle. It cost

€1.80. I had coins in my pocket so started to put my money in, but when I got to my last coin I learned that I only had €1.70. I was 10 cents short and very thirsty.

I thought that maybe I could get money from Elizabeth, but she was too far away and the lounge was so busy that she couldn't see or hear me. I looked around and saw two air stewardesses a few feet away so I asked them if they could lend me 10 cents. They weren't impressed. One of them responded

a little sarcastically, 'What, are you gonna pay it back?'
I have to say that I take many opportunities to lecture
people on the benefits of love and kindness. Here was one.
I said, 'I'll go one better. I'll pay it forward.'

The stewardesses took a confused look at each other and
then at me, and the one who had spoken before said,
'*What?*'

I explained that as I didn't have 10 cents to pay her back,
I'd recognize her kindness by doing something kind for
someone else. That would mean that I would have passed
on her kindness – paid it forward. Someone, somewhere,
would benefit from it.

By now the girls had got interested. They were inspired.
This was a concept they were definitely going to try out in
their own lives.

So the girl gladly gave me 10 cents and I popped it into
the machine. Out came the water, as expected, but then
the 10 cents rolled back out again! I handed it back to the
girl, but she refused to take it. She said that I had committed
to doing something kind for someone and if she took the
10 cents back then she'd be denying someone an act of
kindness. I saw her point.

She suggested that we put the money in a charity box.
There was one just a few feet from us. So she did it and
left me still obliged to do something kind for someone.

My opportunity presented itself a few moments later. The departure lounge was very busy and there were loads of people standing because there weren't enough free seats. I saw an elderly man nearby, looking tired and holding his bag. I placed my own bag on my seat and walked up to him and offered him my seat. At first he said he was fine, but I could tell he wasn't. You know the way we do that? Certainly it's common where I come from. It's an inbuilt reaction to refuse kindness because you don't want to put the person to any trouble.

So I explained that I was just about to board my flight and when I did someone was going to get my seat and I'd rather it was him. After that, he took me up on my offer and I escorted him over to the seat.

So the girl who gave me 10 cents just helped the elderly man to get a seat. Think about it. Maybe I wouldn't have thought to offer my seat otherwise. When you are charged with performing an act of kindness, you are alert to opportunities. You become a source of little miracles in the lives of others. And the more you give, the more you receive. Miracles start to happen in your own life too. They don't happen *to* you, they happen *because* of you.

Be the inspiration

When I was a child we went through times of being so poor that my mum and dad had very little money to feed and clothe me and my sisters. I remember as if it was yesterday my mum making dinner for the six of us. As she was putting the potatoes and vegetables onto the plates, she would remove a potato from her plate and put it onto my dad's, giving him more because he needed the energy for his manual job. Then she'd remove another and put it on my plate or one of my sisters' plates. Then she'd do the same with the vegetables. This would go on until she hardly had any dinner on her own plate.

I don't know if all mums do this. Maybe they do. But I know it made a lasting impression on me and was a constant demonstration of my mum's love for us. It's these small things, or things that seem small to the giver at the time, that make the biggest difference. They are never forgotten. That memory colours much of what I do today and, along with similar childhood experiences, is what inspires me to write about love and kindness.

A few years back when Elizabeth and I had only been together a short time, she used all of the money that she owned at the time to help me out. I was a director of a charity that a few friends and I had started and had no income. Elizabeth was volunteering full time for the charity, so she had no income either, just some savings. I had been paying for a car for almost three years, having bought it when I worked in the pharmaceutical industry. I had three more payments to make and then I could hand it back to the HP company, which you could do after paying 60 per cent of it. Even though Elizabeth had no income, she cleaned out her bank account to do this for me, leaving herself with nothing. Despite my efforts to refuse the money, her determination to help meant that the car was finally paid for. This might have seemed like a small thing to Elizabeth, such is her generosity of spirit, but it was a big thing to me. Acts like this change the world.

Look around you, to family members, friends, work colleagues, people you come into contact with, and allow yourself to be inspired by them. Pay attention to the demonstrations of love and kindness that most of us take for granted. Of course there will be times when their actions are not so kind. We all have slip-ups. But when you look beyond that, at their human spirit, you help to bring out the best in them.

We all have the power to see the spirit inside people, no matter how well it is hidden. So try to see the best in everyone you know, just as you would hope that they would see past some of your own behaviour and see the best in you.

Try to show respect for people too. Show respect for their race and religion. These are the obvious candidates that we hear about. But extend this and show respect for their daily way of life too. There is a multitude of differing beliefs and opinions about lifestyle, politics, food, science and medicine, all over the world.

You don't have to agree with everything another person believes. But you don't need to be nasty or unkind if you disagree. Even if you are more educated or have more information, try to show kindness and respect for where another person is in their life. Chances are your opinions have evolved over the years. Theirs will too. We're all part of the same human family and everyone is on a journey trying to find their way home.

Extend your respect to people who work with or for you. If someone makes a mistake or is not performing to your standards, don't shout at them or treat them disrespectfully. If you need to say something to them, be honest, and do it kindly and respectfully, regardless of their age or level of experience. Don't talk behind their back. That way they will respect you more. And, who knows, the mistake might just turn out for the best in the grander scheme of things. At the very least it has offered you the opportunity to learn to act with kindness and compassion and become a better person – a bigger person.

Being a bigger person is what takes you forward. And it takes a bigger person to be kind than to be firm or tough. It takes a bigger person to show tolerance. It takes a bigger person to show a willingness to communicate and understand rather than criticize and find fault.

Forgive

Also, try to forgive people who have hurt or offended you. In her wonderfully moving book *Left to Tell*, Immaculée Ilibagiza tells her story of how her family, as well as almost a million others, was murdered in the 1994 Rwanda massacres. But on visiting a jail and being confronted by one of the ringleaders, she writes, '[He] was sobbing. I could feel his shame. He looked up at me for only a moment, but our eyes met. I reached out, touched his hands tightly, and quietly said what I'd come to say. "I forgive you."'

Similarly, Christ said, 'Forgive them, Father. For they know not what they do.'

Some people who hurt us really don't realize that what they're doing is wrong or hurtful. Some have chemical deficiencies in their brain that limit their self-control. Others are caught up in pack mentality. Still others are just not able to help themselves. Once they cross a line they can't stop. Some people have been so hurt in the past that they have closed off their feelings of compassion. And, of course, there *are* people who coldly set out to do harm, but there are far fewer of them than there are of the rest.

I'm not trying to make excuses for people's behaviour, only to suggest that most of the hurts we suffer in life are inflicted by people who are either unaware or themselves damaged in some way. Maybe knowing this can help you to forgive – or at least forgive the smaller things. Forgiving the bigger stuff is harder, and no one can really know how you feel, so no one can tell you what you should or shouldn't do. But maybe you can make a start with the smaller stuff – the people who have offended you or said something unkind. If we all made an effort to let the smaller things go then we'd make a big difference in the world.

What are you holding on to today? What pain are you reliving? What weights do you carry on your shoulders?

A really great exercise in forgiveness can all be done in the mind. First make your apologies to the people you have hurt or might have hurt in the past. Think of those people and, in your mind, speak to them and tell them you are sorry for what you said or did. Then think of the people you've talked about behind their back (might take a while for most of us) and even the people you've had unkind thoughts about.

Then move on to forgiving the people who have hurt or offended you, including friends, colleagues, family members and people who've been in your life in the past. Sometimes it can take several attempts to genuinely feel that you've forgiven someone. But when you do, you feel lighter and in some way you also free that person too. After Immaculée said what she came to say, she wrote, 'My heart eased immediately, and I saw the tension release in [his] shoulders.' Sometimes this can take a lifetime, but maybe that's your path.

Have courage

It sometimes takes courage to be a good person and to do the right thing. It's much easier to fall in line, even when you know something is wrong, but this doesn't get anyone anywhere. It's doing the right thing that changes the world. The more people do the right thing, the more the world becomes coloured by the right things. Even simple things like owning up to having been given too much change in a shop makes a difference. Go back in and hand it back. It might take courage to be the miracle, but the rewards are huge.

I've had the good fortune to know many inspirational people in my life, although none of them would think they're inspirational. Make a point of noticing the people around you who are being the miracle, and let yourself be inspired by them. Then you will be an inspiration to others too. Most examples are small ones, but they are miracles all the same.

One of my favourite films is *Bruce Almighty*. Near the end of the film, Bruce, a journalist played by Jim Carrey, has a near-fatal accident and has an NDE. He speaks to God and God says:

> *'A single mom who's working two jobs and still finds time to take her son to soccer practice, that's a miracle. A teenager who says "no" to drugs and "yes" to an education, that's a miracle. People want me to do everything for*

them. What they don't realize is they have the power. You want to see a miracle, son? Be the miracle.'

Do I believe that through the power of our free will, we can create a beautiful world that we'd be proud to bring our children into? Yes, I wholeheartedly do. Maybe it'll take a miracle. If so, then I invite you, today, to be the miracle!

In Closing

We can create the type of world we want by choosing to be an example of what we wish to see. There are forces of destiny that incline our personal lives and the world in a particular direction and maybe these forces will naturally reveal such a magical place. But we have free will to create it for ourselves.

Every thought attracts. So even if destiny were leading us to this wonderful future, our thoughts, words and actions could lead us astray. On the other hand, if the forces of destiny were taking us to hard times, our thoughts, words and actions could change that too.

It's all up to us. We create our destiny.

I have suggested two main ways to ensure the best possible destiny:

1. Count your blessings.
2. Be the miracle.

I believe that this is a simple formula that helps us to find that place inside us that resonates with the soul. When we find it, it begins to colour the climate around us – the mental and emotional climate – and then it filters out into the world. So if we are the miracle, the world will be the miracle too. That's what I choose. What about you? I think our children and our children's children deserve no less. We have a responsibility to pass on to them a world that they can thrive in.

When I was growing up, my mum and dad worked hard to give my three sisters and me some of the things they didn't get. That inspired them. I am inspired now to create a world where all of our children can get some of the things that we didn't get. Maybe we can give them a world of peace, of sharing, of co-operation. Maybe we can give them a world where no one goes hungry, where poverty has been eradicated. Maybe we can give them a world where disease has been eradicated too. Maybe we can give them a world where everyone gets an education.

Will this take a miracle? Maybe. So let's be the miracle. Let's shoot for the stars. Don't you dream of such possibilities? I'll bet you do. You can do it! You only need to start today.

I don't think we've even begun to unleash our power to create such a world. We tie ourselves down by thinking that we are unimportant; that the only people who can make a difference are the ones in power. Well, history has shown us that this is rarely the case. History is filled with stories of people who had a dream and acted on it.

And they changed the world!

References

Chapter 1

For the scientific study of women's menstrual cycles and phases of the moon, see Law, S. P., 'The regulation of menstrual cycle and its relationship to the moon', *Acta. Obstet. Gynecol. Scand.*, 1986, 65(1), 45–8.

For report of the study of the effect of the full moon on self-poisoning, see Buckley, N. A., Whyte, I. M. and Dawson, A. H., 'There are days … and moons: self-poisoning is not lunacy', *Medical Journal of Australia*, 1993, 159(11–12), 786–9 (Abstract). The article is also referenced in Gawande, A., 'E.R. and the triple hex: when a full moon and a lunar eclipse collide with Friday 13th, do more accidents really happen?' (1998). Article on http://www.slate.com/id/2673.

For the opening of oysters and the position of the moon, see Frank A. Brown Jr., 'Persistent activity rhythms in the oyster', *Am. J. Physiol.*, 1954, 178, 510–14.

For information on the research of Michel Gauquelin, see Michel Gauquelin, *Written in the Stars* (The Aquarian Press, 1988). Some of his work is cited in Percy Seymour,

The Scientific Proof of Astrology (Quantum, 1997).

For information on sunspots and sunspot cycles, see http://www.spaceweather.com and http://solarscience. msfc.nasa.gov. The space weather website also gives data on current magnetic storm activity. If you sign up you can receive regular e-mails regarding space weather conditions and magnetic storm activity.

For a report of the prediction of sunspot cycle 24 due to peak around 2012, see http://www.ucar.edu/news/releases/ 2006/sunspot.shtml. It's a 2006 article titled 'Scientists issue unprecedented forecast of next sunspot cycle'. The website is that of the National Center for Atmospheric Research.

For the papers on planetary alignments and magnetic storms, see:

- Blizard, J. B., 'Long-range solar flare prediction', *NASA Contractor Report*, 1969, CR61316
- Jose, P., 'Sun's motion and sunspots', *Astronomical Journal*, 1965, 70, 193–200
- Nelson, J., 'Shortwave radio propagation correlation with planetary positions', *RCA Review*, 1951, cited in Percy Seymour, *The Scientific Proof of Astrology* (Quantum, 1997).

See also:

- Okal, E. and Anderson, D. L., 'On the planetary theory of sunspots', *Nature*, 1975, 253, 511–13
- Wood, K. D., 'Physical sciences: sunspots and planets', *Nature*, 1972, 240, 91–3
- Wood, R. M., 'Comparison of sunspot periods with planetary synodic period resonances', *Nature*, 1975, 255, 312–13.

These three papers discuss the effects of the orbits of the tidal planets (Mercury, Venus, the Earth and Jupiter) on sunspots.

For a really good book on astrology, see Julia and Derek Parker, *Parker's Astrology* (Dorling Kindersley, 1991).

For links to Michael Persinger and some of his research, see http://en.wikipedia.org/wiki/Michael_Persinger.

For Dr Ronald Kay's research on the link between magnetic storms and depression, see http://www.depression.org.uk/information/article_output.php?purpose=1&category=3&curr_page=6.

For the scientific publication, see Kay, R. W., 'Geomagnetic storms: association with incidence of depression as measured by hospital admission', *British Journal of Psychiatry*, 1994, 164, 403–9.

For an excellent summary and citation list of the effects of geomagnetic fields on health, see www.electric-fields.bris.ac.uk/geomagneticfields.pdf. It's a report in PDF format by Jonathan P. Ward and Denis L. Henshaw of the H. H. Wills Physics Laboratories, University of Bristol, UK. The report is called *Geomagnetic Fields, their Fluctuations and Health Effects.*

For the research on the effects of magnetic storms on suicide, see Berk, M., Dodd, S. and Henry, M., 'Do ambient electromagnetic fields affect behaviour? A demonstration of the relationship between geomagnetic storm activity and suicide', *Bioelectromagnetics*, 2006, 27, 151–5.

For effects of magnetic storms on melatonin levels, see:

- Burch, J. B., Reif, J. S. and Yost, M. G., 'Geomagnetic disturbances are associated with reduced nocturnal excretion of melatonin metabolite in humans', *Neuroscience Letters*, 2006, 266, 209–12
- Jozsa, R. *et al.*, 'Chronomics, neuroendocrine feedsidewards and the recording and consulting of nowcasts-forecasts of geomagnetics', *Biomed. Pharmacother.*, 2005, 59, Suppl. 1: S24–30
- Rapaport, S. I. *et al.*, 'Melatonin production in hypertensive patients exposed to magnetic storms', *Terapevticeskij arhiv.*, 2001, 73(12), 29–33
- Semm, P., Schneider, T. and Vollrath, L., 'Effects

of Earth-strength magnetic field on electrical
activity of pineal cells', *Nature*, 1980, 288, 607–8

• Weydahl, A., Sothern, R. B., Cornelissen, G. and
Wetterberg, L., 'Geomagnetic activity influences
the melatonin secretion at latitude 70° N',
Biomed. Pharmacother., 2001, 55, 57–62.

For other biological effects, see:

• Baevsky, R. M. *et al.*, 'Meta-analysed heart rate
variability, exposure to geomagnetic storms, and
the risk of ischemic heart disease', *Scr. Med.
(Brno)*, 1997, 70(4–5), 201–6

• Gurfinkel, Y. I., Liubimov, V. V., Oraevskii, V. N.,
Parafenova, L. M., Iur'ev, A. S., 'The effect of
geomagnetic disturbances in capillary blood flow
in ischemic heart disease patients', *Biofizika*,
1995, 40(4), 793–9

• Gurfinkel, Y. I., Voekov, V. L. Buravlyova., E. V.
and Kondakov, S. E., 'Effect of geomagnetic
storms on the erythrocyte sedimentation rate in
ischemic patients', *Crit. Rev. Biomed. Eng.*, 2001,
29(1), 65–76

• Pikin, D. A., Gurfinkel, Y. I. and Orasvskii, V.
N., 'Effect of geomagnetic disturbances on the
blood coagulation system in patients with
ischemic heart disease and prospects for correction
with medication', *Biofizika*, 1998, 43(4), 617–22.
Note: This paper also showed that aspirin reduced
the negative effect of the magnetic storms.

Some research has indicated that there might be a link between magnetic storms and some instances of cot death (sudden infant death syndrome, SIDS). The evidence is not conclusive, but suggests that more research is required. See the Jonathan P. Ward and Denis L. Henshaw report cited above.

For the effects of magnetic storms on stock returns, see the following internal report by the Federal Reserve Bank of Atlanta: http://www.frbatlanta.org/invoke.cfm?objectid =AFD46B63-2852-4812-BE83E6D0C777F4BF& method=display.

For the study of the blind mole rats' use of the Earth's magnetic field, see Kimchi, T. and Terkel, J., 'Magnetic compass orientation in the blind mole rat *Spalax ehrenbergi*', *Journal of Experimental Biology*, 2001, 204(4), 751–8.

For the monarch butterfly, see Etheredge, J. A., Perez, S. M., Taylor, O. R. and Jander, R., 'Monarch butterflies (*Danaus plexippus L.*) use a magnetic compass for navigation', *Proceedings of the National Academy of Sciences*, 1999, 96(24), 13845–6. See also http://www.science-news.org/pages/sn_arc99/11_27_99/fob7.htm.

For the loggerhead turtle, see Lohmann, K. J. and Lohmann, C. M. F., 'Detection of magnetic field intensity by sea turtles', *Nature*, 1996, 380, 59–61. See also http://www.sciencedaily.com/releaes/2001/10/01101207 3954.htm.

The information about bees and whales was taken from Percy Seymour, *The Scientific Proof of Astrology* (Quantum, 1997). See also http://www.pbs.org/wgbh/nova/magnetic/animals.html.

For birds seeing the Earth's magnetic field, see Ritz, T., Thalau, P., Phillips, J. B., Wiltschko, R. and Wiltschko, W., 'Resonance effects indicate a radical-pair mechanism for avian magnetic compass', *Nature*, 2004, 429, 177–80. See also http://www.sciencedaily.com/releases/2004/05/040514030725.htm.

For other animals' use of the Earth's magnetic field for navigation, here is a short list of articles of interest:

- 'Migratory songbirds have a specialized night-vision brain area' in http://www.sciencedaily.com/releases/2005/05/050523234717.htm
- 'Chickens orient using a magnetic compass' in http://www.sciencedaily.com/releases/2005/08/050825071055.htm
- 'Pigeons can sense the Earth's magnetic field: ability might allow them to return home' in http://www.sciencedaily.com/releases/2004/11/041129100043.htm
- 'Lobsters navigate by magnetism, study says' in http://news.nationalgeographic.com/news/2003/01/0106_030106_lobster.html
- Banks, N. and Srygley, R. B., 'Orientation by

magnetic field in leaf-cutter ants, *Atta colombica* (*Hymenoptera: Formicidae*)', *Ethology*, 2003, 109, 835–46.

The information on Dr Robin Baker and the magnetoreception ability in humans can be found in R. Robin Baker, *Human Navigation and Magnetoreception* (Manchester University Press, 1989).

For the paper showing the onset of labour peaking at certain times, see Cagnacci, A., Soldani, R., Melis, G. B. and Volpe, A., 'Diurnal rhythms of labour and delivery in women: modulation by parity and seasons', *American Journal of Obstetrics & Gynecology*, 1998, 178(1), 140–45.

For information on the Mayans, their civilization, astronomy and prophecies, see Adrian Gilbert and Maurice Cotterell, *The Mayan Prophecies: Unlocking the secrets of a lost civilization* (HarperCollins, 1996).

For information on 2012, see Lawrence E. Joseph, *Apocalypse 2012* (HarperCollins, 2007).

Chapter 2

For the priming experiment using the 'old' words, see Bargh, J. A., Chen, M. and Burrows, L., 'Automaticity of social behaviour: direct effects of trait construction and stereotype activation on action', *Journal of Personality and Social Psychology*, 1996, 71(2), 230–44.

For the Trivial Pursuit priming experiment, see Dijksterhuis, A. and van Knippenberg, A., 'The relation between perception and behaviour, or How to win a game of Trivial Pursuit', *Journal of Personality and Social Psychology*, 1998, 74(4), 865–77.

For the paper on the Friday 13th study in London, see Scanlon, T. J., Luben, R. N., Scanlon, F. L. and Singleton, N., 'Is Friday 13th bad for your health?', *British Medical Journal*, 1993, 307(6919), 1584–6.

For the Finland study, see Nayha, S., 'Traffic deaths and superstition on Friday 13th', *American Journal of Psychiatry*, 2002, 159(12), 2110–1.

For a good description of the planets, their personalities and the myths of the constellations, see:

- Julia and Derek Parker, *Parker's Astrology* (Dorling Kindersley, 1991)
- Russell Grant, *You Can Change your Life* (Ebury Press, 2006).

For the fMRI study at Bastyr University, see Standish, L. J. Johnson, L. C., Richards, T. and Kozak, L., 'Evidence of correlated functional MRI signals between distant human brains', *Alternative Therapies in Health and Medicine*, 2003, 9, 122–8.

See also:

- Standish, L., J., Kozak, L., Johnson, L. C. and Richards, T., 'Electroencephalographic evidence of correlated event-related signals between the brains of spatially and sensory isolated human subjects', *Journal of Alternative and Complementary Medicine*, 2004, 10, 307–14
- Wackermann, J., Seiter, C., Keibel, H. and Walach, H., 'Correlations between brain electrical activities of two spatially separated human subjects', *Neuroscience Letters*, 2003, 336, 60–64.

These studies were reported and described, along with other similar studies, in Dean Radin, *Entangled Minds* (Pocket Books, 2006).

For information on the zif-268 gene and an excellent summary of the evidence for the effects of thoughts and emotions on DNA, see Ernest L. Rossi, *The Psychobiology of Gene Expression* (Norton, 2002).

Chapter 3

For a good paper on epigenetics and the effects of the Dutch famine, see Pray, Leslie A., 'Epigenetics: Genome, meet your environment', *The Scientist*, 2004, 18(13), 14. You can read it online at: http://www.the-scientist.com/article/display/14798.

For the increased incidence of heart disease, see Roseboom, T. J. *et al.*, 'Coronary heart disease after pre-natal exposure to the Dutch famine, 1944–45', *Heart*, 2000, 84(6), 595–8.

For related papers concerning the Dutch famine and the transgenerational effects, see:

- Lumey, L. H., 'Decreased birth weights in infants after maternal *in utero* exposure to the Dutch famine of 1944–45', *Paediatr. Perinat. Epidemiol.*, 1992, 6(2), 240–53
- Lumey, L. H. and van Poppel, F. W. A., 'The Dutch famine of 1944–45: mortality and morbidity in past and present generations', *Social History of Medicine*, 1994, 7(2), 229–46

For the effects of parents' and grandparents' diets on the health of offspring, see Kaati, G., Bygren, L. O. and Edvinsson, S., 'Cardiovascular and diabetes mortality determined by nutrition during parents' and grandparents' slow growth period', *European Journal of Human Genetics*, 2002, 10(11), 682–8.

For a definition of epigenetics and some general information, see http://www.epigenome.eu, which is the website of the Epigenome Network of Excellence.

For a simple, accessible feature on epigenetics that appeared on a UK TV programme called *Horizon*, see http://www.bbc.co.uk/sn/tvradio/programmes/horizon/ghostgenes.shtml.

To read about the effects of the mother's love on rats, see the following article in the *Guardian* newspaper: http://www.guardian.co.uk/genes/article/0,,2012408,00.html. The scientific reference is Weaver, I. C. G. et al., 'The transcription factor nerve growth factor-inducible protein A mediates epigenetic programming: altering epigenetic marks by immediate-early genes', *Journal of Neuroscience*, 2007, 27(7), 1756–68.

For the work showing the effect of toxins four generations on, see Anway, M. D., Leathers, C. and Skinner, M. K., 'Endocrine disruptor vinclozolin induced epigenetic transgenerational adult-onset disease', *Endocrinology*, 2006, 147(12), 5515–23.

See also:

- Anway, M. D., Cupp, A. S., Uzumcu, M. and Skinner, M. K., 'Epigenetic transgenerational actions of endocrine disruptors and male fertility', *Science*, 2005, 308(5727), 1466–9
- Zoeller, R. T., 'Endocrine disruptors: do family lines carry an epigenetic record of previous generations' exposures?', *Endocrinology*, 2006, 147(12), 5513–14.

The study on the agouti gene was reported in Bruce Lipton's *The Biology of Belief* (Mountain of Love/Elite Books, 2005). It is an excellent book that gives accessible information on epigenetics and the effects of the environment on the cell and gene.

The ten-generational effect on the fruit fly can be read in the article 'Epigenetics: Genome, meet your environment' cited above. The source paper is Rutherford, S. L. and Lindquist, S., 'Hsp90 as a capacitor for morphological evolution', *Nature*, 1998, 396, 336–43.

For information on the biochemistry of epigenetics, which is often the result of the methylation of DNA, see Kling, J., 'Put the blame on methylation', *The Scientist*, 2003, 17(12), 27.

The report of the 1980 Soviet Olympic Squad was taken from Michael Talbot, *The Holographic Universe* (HarperCollins, 1991). It also provides some excellent information on multiple personality disorder.

For more information on multiple personality disorder, see:

- Goleman, D., 'Probing the enigma of multiple personality'. This is a *New York Times* article. See http://query.nytimes.com/gst/fullpage.html?res =940DEFD61238F93BA15755C0A96E948 260&sec=health&spon=&pagewanted=1

- Moleman, N., Hulscher, J. B. F., van der Hart, O. and Scheepstra, G. L., 'The effect of multiple personality disorder on anesthesia: a case report', *Dissociation*, 1991, 7(1), 197–200.

The poison ivy placebo report is taken from Herbert Benson, MD, *Timeless Healing* (Simon & Schuster, 1996).

Chapter 4

For the Pim van Lommel study, see Van Lommel, P., van Wees, R., Meyers, V. and Elfferich, I., 'Near-death experience in survivors of cardiac arrest: a prospective study in the Netherlands', *The Lancet*, 2001, 358, 2039–45.

For a good source of information about NDEs, see: http://www.near-death.com.

The Gallup poll results were taken from Raymond A. Moody, *The Light Beyond* (Rider, 2005). This book is also an excellent source of information about the scientific validation of life after death. It gives information that overcomes some of the sceptical proposals that it is just hallucination.

The mind-reading news report about the use of fMRI technology can be read at http://news.bbc.co.uk/1/hi/health/6346069.stm.

Dr Michael Sabom's study is discussed in his book,

Recollections of Death: A Medical Investigation (Harper & Row, 1982).

For life on the other side, see:

- Sylvia Browne, *Life on the Other Side* (Piatkus Books, 2000)
- Deepak Chopra, *Life After Death: The Burden of Proof* (Harmony Books, 2006)
- Michael Newton, *Destiny of Souls* (Llewellyn Publications, 2000)
- Gordon Smith, *Stories from the Other Side* (Hay House, 2006)
- Neale Donald Walsch, *Home with God* (Hodder & Stoughton, 2006)
- Brian Weiss, *Many Lives, Many Masters* (Fireside, 1988).

Chapter 5

For some of the research conducted by the PEAR Group at Princeton University, see Dunne, B. J. and Jahn, R. G., 'Consciousness, information, and living systems', *Cellular and Molecular Biology*, 2005, 51, 703–14.

For some 'time' experiments, see:

- Braud, W., 'Wellness implications of retroactive intentional influence: exploring an outrageous hypothesis', *Alternative Therapies*, 2000, 6(1),

37–48. This paper summarizes a number of these retroactive experiments.

- Leibovici, L., 'Effects of remote, retroactive intercessory prayer on outcomes in patients with bloodstream infection: randomized controlled trial', *British Medical Journal*, 2001, 323, 1450–51.

David Bohm's work on implicate and explicate order can be found in his book, *Wholeness and the Implicate Order* (Routledge, 1980).

The following three books are excellent accessible sources of information on quantum physics and contain descriptions of the Many Worlds theory:

- Jim Al-Khalili, *Quantum: A Guide for the Perplexed* (Weidenfield & Nicholson, 2003)
- Brian Greene, *The Fabric of the Cosmos* (Penguin, 2004)
- John Gribbin, *In Search of Schrödinger's Cat* (Corgi, 1985).

Chapter 6

Rupert Sheldrake has conducted many studies on sensing who is on the other end of the telephone, knowing when someone is staring at you and other similar effects. The study I described can be read at http://www.mind-energy.net/archives/121-Telephone-telepathy-experiments-of-rupert-sheldrake.html.

The dream experiments and the EEG experiments were taken from Dean Radin's *Entangled Minds*, cited above.

Chapter 7

For the law of attraction, see:

- Rhonda Byrne, *The Secret* (Simon & Schuster, 2006). See also the DVD.
- Esther and Jerry Hicks, *Ask and It Is Given* (Hay House, 2005)
- Esther and Jerry Hicks, *The Amazing Power of Deliberate Intent* (Hay House, 2006)
- Esther and Jerry Hicks, *The Law of Attraction: The Basics of the Teachings of Abraham* (Hay House, 2006).

Chapter 8

Brian Weiss's future scenarios can be found in his book *Same Soul, Many Bodies*, (Free Press, 2004).

A report on Lonnie Thomson's discovery can be read at http://researchnews.osu.edu/archive/5200event.htm.
For a metaphysical view of the collective creation of mass events, see:

- Jane Roberts, *Seth Speaks* (Prentice Hall, 1972)
- Jane Roberts, *The Nature of Personal Reality* (Prentice Hall, 1974)

- Jane Roberts, *The Individual and the Nature of Mass Events* (Prentice Hall, 1981).

To read about indigo children, see the article on the online encyclopaedia Wikipedia: http://en.wikipedia.org/wiki/Indigo_children.

Chapter 9

For more on the point of life and some spiritual approaches and philosophies, I would recommend the following books that I have found helpful:

- Dr Wayne Dyer, *Inspiration* (Hay House, 2006)
- Dr David R. Hawkins, *Power vs Force* (Veritas Publishing, 1995)
- Eckhart Tolle, *The Power of Now* (New World Library, 1999).

Chapter 10

For an article on criminal behaviour and the lack of important chemicals in the brain, see Greenspan, P. S., 'Genes, electrotransmitters, and free will', paper from D. Wasserman and R. Wachbroit (eds), *Genetics and Criminal Behaviour: Methods, Meanings and Morals* (Cambridge University Press, 2001).

For photographs of the brain scans of the prefrontal lobes of a violent vs a non-violent person, see Joseph Chilton Pearce, *The Biology of Transcendence* (Park Street Press, 2002).

For the studies on the use of EPA to treat post-natal depression, see David Servan-Schreiber, *Healing without Freud or Prozac* (Rodale International Ltd, 2005).

Further Reading

The following are some books that you may find useful in furthering your knowledge and understanding of some of the concepts in this book.

Astrology and magnetic effects

R. Robin Baker, *Human Navigation and Magnetoreception*, Manchester University Press, 1989

Jude Currivan, *The Wave*, O Books, 2005

Jude Currivan, *The 8th Chakra*, Hay House, 2006

Michel Gauquelin, *Written in the Stars*, The Aquarian Press, 1988

Russell Grant, *You Can Change Your Life*, Ebury Press, 2006

Julia and Derek Parker, *Parker's Astrology*, Dorling Kindersley, 1991

Dr Percy Seymour, *The Scientific Proof of Astrology*, Quantum, 1997

Penny Thornton, *The Forces of Destiny: Reincarnation, Karma and Astrology*, The Aquarian Press, 1990

Life after death

Sylvia Browne, *Life on the Other Side*, Piatkus Books, 2000

Deepak Chopra, *Life After Death: The Burden of Proof*, Harmony Books, 2006

Raymond A. Moody, *The Light Beyond*, Bantam, 1989

Michael Newton, *Journey of Souls*, Llewellyn Publications, 1994

Michael Newton, *Destiny of Souls*, Llewellyn Publications, 2000

Michael Sabom, *Recollections of Death: A Medical Investigation*, Harper & Row, 1982

Gordon Smith, *The Unbelievable Truth*, Hay House, 2004

Gordon Smith, *Through My Eyes*, Hay House, 2006

Gordon Smith, *Stories from the Other Side*, Hay House, 2006

Neale Donald Walsch, *Home with God*, Hodder & Stoughton, 2006

Dr Brian Weiss, *Many Lives, Many Masters*, Fireside, 1988

Dr Brian Weiss, *Same Soul, Many Bodies*, Piatkus Books, 2004

The law of attraction and creating reality

Rhonda Byrne, *The Secret*, Atria Books/Beyond Words, 2006

Rhonda Byrne, *The Secret* DVD, Prime Time Productions, 2006

Wayne Dyer, *The Power of Intention*, Hay House, 2005

Esther and Jerry Hicks, *Ask and It Is Given*, Hay House, 2005

Esther and Jerry Hicks, *The Amazing Power of Deliberate Intent*, Hay House, 2006

Esther and Jerry Hicks, *The Law of Attraction: The Basics of the Teachings of Abraham*, Hay House, 2006

Jane Roberts, *Seth Speaks*, Prentice Hall, 1972

Jane Roberts, *The Nature of Personal Reality*, Prentice Hall, 1974

Jane Roberts, *The Individual and the Nature of Mass Events*, Prentice Hall, 1981

Sandra Anne Taylor, *Quantum Success*, Hay House, 2006

Inspirational and spiritual

Dr Wayne Dyer, *Inspiration: Your Ultimate Calling*, Hay House, 2006

Dr David R. Hawkins, *Power vs Force*, Hay House, 1998

Eckhart Tolle, *The Power of Now*, New World Library, 1999

Albert Villoldo, *The Four Insights*, Hay House, 2006

Biology, connectedness and quantum physics

Jim Al-Khalili, *Quantum: A Guide for the Perplexed*, Weidenfield & Nicholson, 2003

Herbert Benson, MD, *Timeless Healing*, Simon & Schuster, 1996

David Bohm, *Wholeness and the Implicate Order*, Routledge, 1980

Jude Currivan, *The Wave*, O Books, 2005

Jude Currivan, *The 8th Chakra*, Hay House, 2006

Brian Greene, *The Fabric of the Cosmos*, Penguin, 2004

John Gribbin, *In Search of Schrödinger's Cat*, Corgi, 1985

Bruce Lipton, PhD, *The Biology of Belief*, Mountain of Love/Elite Books, 2005

Lynne McTaggart, *The Intention Experiment*, HarperElement, 2007

Joseph Chilton Pearce, *The Biology of Transcendence*, Park Street Press, 2002

Dean Radin, *Entangled Minds*, Paraview/Pocket Books, 2006

Ernest L. Rossi, *The Psychobiology of Gene Expression*, Norton, 2002

David Servan-Schreiber, *Healing without Freud or Prozac*, Rodale International Ltd, 2005

Michael Talbot, *The Holographic Universe*, HarperCollins, 1991

2012

Lawrence E. Joseph, *Apocalypse 2012*, Morgan Road Books, 2007

Adrian Gilbert and Maurice Cotterell, *The Mayan Prophecies*, HarperCollins, 1996

Others

Malcolm Gladwell, *Blink*, Little, Brown and Company, 2005

Dan Millman, *The Life You Were Born to Live*, H. J. Kramer, 1993

About the Author

David R. Hamilton gained a first-class honours degree in chemistry, specializing in biological and medical chemistry, and a PhD in organic chemistry before going on to be a scientist in the pharmaceutical industry in 1995. Over the next four years he also served as an athletics coach and team manager for one of the UK's top athletics clubs. He left both roles in 1999 and has since worked as a motivational speaker, co-founded an international relief charity, co-organized a nine-day, 24-event festival of peace called Spirit Aid and worked as a college lecturer in both chemistry and ecology. He has been featured on TV and radio and been the subject of national newspaper articles. He spends most of his time writing, giving talks and leading workshops.

For additional information, including details of events, lectures and workshops, see: **www.drdavidhamilton.com**

We hope you enjoyed this Hay House book.
If you would like to receive a free catalogue featuring additional
Hay House books and products, or if you would like information
about the Hay Foundation, please contact:

Hay House UK Ltd
292B Kensal Rd • London W10 5BE
Tel: (44) 20 8962 1230; Fax: (44) 20 8962 1239
www.hayhouse.co.uk

✻✻✻

Published and distributed in the United States of America by:
Hay House, Inc. • PO Box 5100 • Carlsbad, CA 92018-5100
Tel.: (1) 760 431 7695 or (1) 800 654 5126;
Fax: (1) 760 431 6948 or (1) 800 650 5115
www.hayhouse.com

Published and distributed in Australia by:
Hay House Australia Ltd • 18/36 Ralph St • Alexandria NSW 2015
Tel.: (61) 2 9669 4299; Fax: (61) 2 9669 4144
www.hayhouse.com.au

Published and distributed in the Republic of South Africa by:
Hay House SA (Pty) Ltd • PO Box 990 • Witkoppen 2068
Tel./Fax: (27) 11 706 6612 • orders@psdprom.co.za

Published and distributed in India by:
Hay House Publishers India • Muskaan Complex • Plot No.3
B-2 • Vasant Kunj • New Delhi – 110 070.
Tel.: (91) 11 41761620; Fax: (91) 11 41761630.
contact@hayhouseindia.co.in

Distributed in Canada by:
Raincoast • 9050 Shaughnessy St • Vancouver, BC V6P 6E5
Tel.: (1) 604 323 7100; Fax: (1) 604 323 2600

✻✻✻

Sign up via the Hay House UK website to receive the Hay House
online newsletter and stay informed about what's going on with
your favourite authors. You'll receive bimonthly announcements
about discounts and offers, special events, product highlights,
free excerpts, giveaways, and more!
www.hayhouse.co.uk